HOME BREW BEER

HOME BREW BEER

MASTER THE ART OF BREWING YOUR OWN BEER

GREG HUGHES

CONTENTS

FOREWORD

Without a doubt, brewing your own beer and enjoying the fruits of your labors is one of the most satisfying pastimes there is.

My own career in the brewing industry grew out of a strong interest in home brewing. As a young boy, I was fascinated by everything related to beer and brewing—perhaps fueled by stories of my grandfather (who I never met) who was the head brewer of a local brewery. On family car trips, I would keep a log of every pub we passed, noting down the breweries whose names adorned each pub sign. When I started brewing my own beer, I sought to re-create the beers produced by those breweries, honing my recipes to get as close to the originals as possible. With each brew, I learned new techniques and made subtle adjustments. I made mistakes, too—and certainly this book would have helped me avoid them—but even mistakes can have serendipitous results. The first golden beer I brewed, for example, was the result of forgetting to add crystal malt to what should have been a darker ale.

I am as excited about brewing today as I was 33 years ago when I produced my first batch. As you prepare your own beer, whether using malt extract or more complex methods, you are bound to feel a similar sense of excitement, especially as the moment of truth arrives and—having waited patiently for it to ferment and condition—you can finally taste your brew.

Brewing your own beer at home is relatively simple and extremely rewarding. With a good cleanliness regime, careful control of temperature, and the freshest ingredients, you should be able to produce beer that is at least equal, if not superior, to anything produced by professional brewers. You may even decide to re-create abandoned beers and styles that may not have been produced commercially for generations. What is certain is that with so many hop varieties, malt variations, and yeast strains available, the possibilities for experimenting with different flavors are endless.

My career has always been driven by the simple joy of producing special, well-crafted beers. Whether you are brewing for your own consumption or are hoping to bask in the compliments of others, I hope this book will help you get as much enjoyment out of brewing as I do.

Forever thirsty,

Keith Bott
Managing Director of Titanic Brewery
and former Chairman of the Society of Independent Brewers

INTRODUCTION

If you enjoy drinking beer, then home brewing is the perfect hobby. Not only will you have the sense of satisfaction that comes from producing your own great-tasting beer, but you will also be able to create any beer style you like—including those not readily available commercially.

FUN, FRUGAL, AND FRIENDLY

Home brewing is relatively easy and can work out at a fraction of the cost of buying beer in the store. The chances are, of course, that you will want to reinvest any savings you make, perhaps by buying new equipment. Even so, you should still be able to break even, which is not a bad return for such an enjoyable and fulfilling hobby. As well as being cost-effective, home brewing is a particularly unselfish interest, since there are always plenty of delicious samples to offer around. In fact, you will probably produce more beer than you can hope to drink—so the more the merrier!

HOME-BREW BASICS

Making beer from a kit is no more difficult than preparing a premade meal—and the results can be truly impressive. With the minimum of fuss, you can make, ferment, and barrel a surprisingly good batch of beer. While many home brewers are content with this approach, if you are reading this book, you are probably seeking something more involved. You'll be happy to know that with just a little extra effort, the possibilities for producing professional and custom beers are almost endless.

MALT-EXTRACT BREWING

The next logical step up the home-brew ladder is to produce beer using malt extract. This is still a relatively straightforward process requiring minimal equipment but one that allows you to experiment with a wider range of ingredients, all the time gaining in confidence. The satisfaction of following a recipe and creating a beer using raw ingredients adds so much to the final product. Using fresh hops, for example, makes a huge difference to the quality of the finished beer.

HONING YOUR SKILLS

Sooner or later, though, you will want to try your hand at the full-mash (or all-grain) method—the "holy grail" of home brewing. There is an art to full-mash brewing that takes more time, research and practice, and you should think of it as an ongoing quest. As you temper and hone your skills, however, the quality of your brews will continue to improve. Just as importantly, you will be able to produce consistently good results and be able to brew exactly the type of beer you had intended to brew at the outset. Many professional craft brewers started their journey as home brewers, honing their skills with small batches before scaling up; this means some of the best breweries in the world owe their existence to home brewing.

EXPLODING SOME MYTHS

You may have heard various home-brew horror stories involving exploding bottles and upset stomachs, or you may have been put off by a bad experience in the past. Exploding bottles are a possibility, of course, but an improbable one if you follow the instructions carefully—and beer is unlikely to make you sick since the alcohol will kill off most forms of bacteria. Today, the quality and availability of home-brew ingredients are better than they have ever been, and there is a wealth of information, advice, and support available from local and online home-brew clubs and groups—places where like-minded brewers share tips and advice. What's more, the growing selection of well-organized home-brewing competitions allow eager home brewers to get valuable feedback on their beer, enabling them to improve their brewing skills.

SOMETHING FOR EVERYONE

In this book, I have tried to cover as much ground as possible without getting too caught up in the details. Whole books have been written about yeast, for example, or brewing one particular style of beer, but I believe it is far better to master the basic techniques and methods first, before specializing in any one area.

The recipes in this book cover every major style of beer, so you should be able to find the perfect lager, ale, wheat beer, or "mixed style" for you. Some recipes are more difficult to brew than others, but you should simply regard these as a challenge. As with all crafts, the more care and effort you put in, the better the results will be, so don't worry if you don't get it quite right every time—your beer will still taste good.

I hope you enjoy making these beers and that you find the recipes appealing and inspiring. Home brewing is one of the best hobbies around and one that I am sure you will enjoy for many years to come—sandals and beard are optional!

Greg Hughes

INTRODUCTION

A BRIEF **HISTORY** OF **BREWING**

Beer production has a long and fascinating history that can be traced back millennia—from the ancient plains of Mesopotamia to the current trend for home brewing worldwide.

7000BCE—Nomadic hunter-gatherers in Mesopotamia (present-day Iraq) **grow and harvest an ancient form of grain**, which is thought to have been used to make an early form of beer.

Pottery chips found in a Neolithic village at the Jiahu site in China contain **traces of compounds found in alcoholic drinks.**

1100–1200s—Commercial hop cultivation begins in northern Germany, followed by the export of hopped beer.

1710—The use of **bittering agents other than hops is banned** by Parliament in England to secure revenue for a hop tax. As a result, hops become the dominant bittering agent in beer throughout the western world.

822CE—Abbot Adalhard from the Benedictine monastery at Corbie in northern France writes a series of statutes covering the running of the monastery, which includes gathering sufficient hops for making beer—**the first documented link between hops and brewing.**

1516—The Beer Purity Law or "Reinheitsgebot" is established in Bavaria. It states that barley, hops, and pure water are the only ingredients allowed in the brewing process. It doesn't extend to the rest of Germany until 1906.

| 7000BCE | 4300BCE | 822 CE | 1040 | 1100-1200s | 1412 | 1516 | 1587 | 1710 |

4300BCE—Babylonian clay tablets dating from this period include details of a **recipe for an alcoholic drink made with grain.**

1040—The first commercial brewery is founded in Weihenstephan Abbey, Bavaria, where the process of brewing becomes a commercial venture by the monks.

Across Europe throughout the Middle Ages, beer becomes one of the most popular drinks. As it is boiled prior to fermentation, it is a safe source of hydration at a time when most water sources are unclean. Its calorie content also makes it an important source of nutrition.

1587—Colonist settlers in Virginia **brew their first batches of beer** (although they still send back to England for more).

1412—The earliest record of **hopped beer** being brewed in England.

Hopped English ale

1810—A festival to celebrate **the marriage of Crown Prince Ludwig** is held in Munich, Germany, which goes on to become the famous **Oktoberfest beer festival**.

Fresh hop cones

1950s—During summer vacation in the UK, up to **10,000 people,** including whole streets of families, leave London for the hop fields of Kent to **pick hops for the local breweries**.

1979—Following an omission during the lifting of Prohibition in the US in 1933, **home brewing is finally legalized** thanks to the Cranston Bill.

1857—French chemist Louis Pasteur discovers that **yeast is responsible for alcoholic fermentation**. This advancement allows brewers to control fermentation, leading to better-quality beers.

1971—English journalists Michael Hardman, Graham Lees, Bill Mellor, and Jim Makin discuss setting up a **consumer organization for beer drinkers**, which goes on to become the Campaign for Real Ale (CAMRA).

1810	1842	1857	1919	1950s	1963	1971	1979	1990s–PRESENT

1919—The 18th Amendment to the US Constitution marks **the start of Prohibition**, which outlaws the sale, manufacture, and transportation of alcohol—including home brewed beer.

1963—British politician Reggie Maudling **lifts taxation on home brewing** and removes the requirement for a license. As a result, home brewing is boosted and grows in popularity during the 1970s.

1990s–PRESENT—**The home brewing world starts to expand** rapidly with a whole range of kits and ingredients coming onto the market.

Today, there is a renewed surge of interest in home brewing, with UK-based manufacturers Muntons selling more than 500,000 kits in 2012, twice as many as in 2007.

Glass of Pilsner

1842—The first **golden lager is produced in Pilsen**, Bohemia. It is a popular style now brewed worldwide.

THE **CRAFT-BEER REVOLUTION**

The global beer market may still be dominated by large breweries, but in the past decade, there has been a rise in the number of artisan breweries producing craft beers.

9,500 BREWERIES were active in Europe in 2018—that's 6,000 more than in 2008

250 CRAFT BREWERIES are located in Canada's Ontario province alone, up from 70 in 2013

25 CRAFT BREWERIES PER 1M PEOPLE in the UK—more than any other country in the world

2.3 BILLION GALLONS (8.7 billion liters) of beer were consumed in Germany in 2016

4.4 MILLION GALLONS (16.6M liters) of craft beer were sold in Mexico in 2017

1.1 MILLION AMERICANS brew their own beer

4,750 CRAFT BREWERIES were operating in the US in 2017

1 MILLION GALLONS (3.7M liters) of craft beer are produced per year in Pennsylvania alone

91% INCREASE IN THE NUMBER OF BREWERIES registered in Brazil between 2014 and 2017

IN 2017,
94%
OF ALL BREWERIES
WORLDWIDE WERE
CRAFT BREWERIES

**$28
BILLION**
was the value of
the Chinese beer
market in 2018

CRAFT BEER
MADE UP
5%
OF ALL BEER
CONSUMPTION
in China in 2018,
up from 0.3% in 2016

**300
CRAFT
BREWERIES**
are currently
operating in Japan

WHAT IS A CRAFT BEER?

A craft beer is any beer produced by a small, independent brewery For example, to label its product "craft beer" in the US, a brewery must produce less than 6 million barrels of beer each year (or less than 3 percent of the US beer market) and must be at least 75 percent owned by the brewer. Craft brewers specialize in attention to detail and produce beers often considered to be far superior to their mass-produced counterparts. While craft brewers do not have the big marketing budgets of the market leaders, they are freer to produce small batches of naturally carbonated, chemical-free beer—something the larger breweries would not find commercially viable.

**200%
GROWTH**
in the Australian
craft-beer industry
between 2011
and 2018

FROM **GRAIN** TO **GLASS**

The brewing process involves steeping a starch—typically malted cereal grains—in water, adding hops for bitterness, flavor, and aroma, and then fermenting the resulting wort with yeast.

1. PREPARING

Every piece of equipment that comes into contact with the beer must be thoroughly cleaned and sterilized (see pp44–45), as any stray bacteria will ruin the brew. Use sterilizing agents and a bottle-cleaning brush.

2. MASHING

The mash (see p57) is the process by which the starches in the malted grains are converted into fermentable sugars. The grains are steeped in hot (but not boiling) water to produce a sweet liquid called the wort.

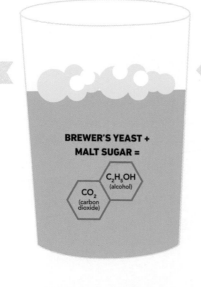

**BREWER'S YEAST +
MALT SUGAR =**

C_2H_5OH
(alcohol)

CO_2
(carbon
dioxide)

6. FERMENTING

The cooled wort is transferred to a fermenter and the yeast is pitched, or added (see pp60–61). The fermenter lid is closed, an airlock fitted, and the wort left to ferment at the specified temperature for about a week. During this time, the sugars in the wort are converted into alcohol.

7. PRIMING AND RACKING

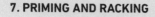

Once fermentation is complete, priming sugar is added to condition the beer and add carbonation. The beer is then racked (transferred) to a storage container, such as a barrel or bottles, and left to condition.

3. SPARGING

The sparge (see p58) involves adding a fine spray of water to the surface of the grain to rinse out the fermentable sugars. The mash tun is drained and the sweet wort transferred to the boiler.

4. BOILING

The wort is then vigorously boiled (see p59) for an hour or more, and hops are added at various intervals. The boil sterilizes the wort and allows the hops to impart bitterness, flavor, and aroma.

5. COOLING

After the boil, the wort must be cooled (see p59) to fermentation temperature (about 68˚F/20˚C)—if the wort is too hot, the yeast cells will be killed when it is added. A rapid cool reduces the chance of bacterial contamination and off-flavors in the beer.

8. CONDITIONING

Depending on the style of beer and the particular recipe, it will need to be left to condition for at least two weeks at the required temperature. This allows the beer to clear and lets the flavors mature.

9. SERVING

After conditioning, the beer is ready to be tasted. The priming sugar will add fizz, but if the brew is too flat, move it to a warm place for a few days and try again. If it is too lively, try chilling it before you pour.

INGREDIENTS

MALT

This is cereal grain that has been allowed to germinate during a process known as malting. Malting activates enzymes that enable starches in the grain to be converted into fermentable sugars.

Barley is the most common grain used to produce malt for brewing. It is naturally high in enzymes and so has the potential to produce high quantities of fermentable sugar. Malted wheat and rye are also widely used in brewing.

There are three varieties of barley: two-row, four-row, and six-row, which refers to the arrangements of kernels around the grain shaft. Two-row barley is the most common variety used for brewing, as it is low in protein and produces more fermentable sugars.

THE MALTING PROCESS

Malt is produced in a building known as a maltings or malt house. Here, the grains are steeped in water, which causes them to absorb moisture and begin to sprout. When the rootlets have grown sufficiently, the grain is dried with warm air to halt any further growth. It is then "tumbled" to remove the rootlets.

Roasting the grains

Once the rootlets have been removed, the grains are roasted to create different types of malts—the higher the roasting temperature, the darker the malt and more intense the flavors. Lightly roasted malts have a high enzymatic (or diastatic) power and so produce lots of fermentable sugar when mixed with hot water during the mash (see p57). Highly roasted malts, on the other hand, have less diastatic power and

produce little or no fermentable sugar. These malts add color, flavor, and aroma to a beer.

Floor malting

Traditionally, after steeping, the grains are spread out across the floor of the maltings to dry. There they are turned by hand using large rakes, which prevents mold from forming and ensures even drying. In the 1940s, industrial techniques were developed to improve the efficiency of the malting process, enabling the production of much larger batches of malt. The traditional method is still considered to produce the best malts, although the practice is rare and malts produced in this way are generally too expensive for commercial brewers.

Crushing the grains

The malting process produces whole malt grains, which must be crushed before adding to the mash (crushing the husks activates the enzymes inside the grains by exposing them to water; these enzymes then break down the starch into fermentable sugars). Most home-brew suppliers sell precrushed malts for convenience, but you can buy whole grains and crush them yourself if you prefer. The process can be messy and time-consuming, but it will ensure that you are using the freshest grains. Once crushed, store them in an airtight container, where they will keep for a few months.

Whole malt grains

COLOR RATING CHART

The color of a malt—and the hue of a finished beer—is measured using one of three internationally recognized scales: the European Brewing Convention (EBC)—the scale used in the recipes in this book, the Standard Reference Method (SRM), and Degrees Lovibond (°L), the original scale developed by Joseph Williams Lovibond in 1883. SRM is approximately equal to °L; EBC is equal to SRM multiplied by 1.97.

COLOR			
EBC	4	6	8
SRM/LOVIBOND	2	3	4
BEER STYLE	Light lager	Weissbier	Witbier

BASE MALTS

These are lightly roasted malts that make up the majority of the grain bill in a recipe and provide most of the fermentable sugars.

Pale base malts

Use Pilsner and lager base malts for very pale lagers and ales. For other ales and darker beers, use pale malts such as Maris Otter and Halcyon.

Darker-roasted base malts

Slightly darker-roasted base malts, such as Munich and Vienna, will provide higher malt flavors, as well as lots of fermentable sugars.

Wheat malt

In addition to producing fermentable sugars, wheat also produces protein, which aids head retention and can add a hazy finish to the beer. Wheat can be difficult to use in the mash.

Rye malt

Less common than either barley or wheat malt, you can use rye to introduce spicy notes to a beer. Like wheat, it can be difficult to mash, so use only in small quantities.

Pale base malt

Wheat malt

SPECIALITY MALTS

These malts are all specially roasted for use in small quantities in the mash to add flavor, color, and aroma. Unlike base malts, they contribute relatively few fermentable sugars.

Caramel malts

Also known as crystal malts, there are a range of caramel malts available, each heated to different temperatures. They introduce honey, caramel, and toffee flavors.

Amber malt

A type of roasted malt with a light, dry, biscuity flavor, amber malt adds a dark amber color to ales and porters. Use only in small quantities.

Roasted malts

These darker-roasted malts have little or no fermentable sugar but provide complex colors, flavors, and aromas.

Caramel malt

Amber malt

Roasted malt

12	16	20	26	33	39	47	57	69	79	138
6	8	10	13	17	20	24	29	35	40	70
Belgian blonde ale	Honey ale	Pale ale		Mild			Black lager		Coffee stout	Imperial stout

ADJUNCTS AND SUGARS

For some beer styles, you will need to use grains other than malted barley (see pp20–21), as well as other fermentable sugars. These adjuncts and sugars all impart particular flavor characteristics.

TORRIFIED WHEAT
This is unmalted wheat that is gently cooked, then rolled to form a flaked grain. It adds a distinctive wheat flavor and increases the head retention of a beer.

SPELT
A close relative of wheat, spelt is a malted grain that imparts a delightful aroma and flavor. Use in small quantities as it can be overpowering.

FLAKED RICE
A common and cost-effective adjunct in American- and Japanese-style light lagers, rice produces particularly crisp and dry beers with minimal flavor.

ROASTED BARLEY
This is a very dark unmalted grain similar to black malt (see p24) but with a less astringent bitterness. It introduces coffee notes that are ideal for stouts and porters.

FLAKED OATS
Easier to use than whole or rolled oats as they don't need to be cooked beforehand, flaked oats add a smooth, silky creaminess. Use in New England IPAs, stouts, and porters.

FLAKED CORN
Also known as flaked maize, this is one of the most commonly used adjuncts. It produces very light beers with a subtle cornlike character and neutral aftertaste.

MALT EXTRACT

This is the fermentable sugar from malted barley (see pp20–21) in concentrated form. Once rehydrated, it can be boiled with hops to create a fermentable wort, or used in the same way as sugar to increase the original gravity, and for use in priming (see p64).

Malt extract is prone to oxidizing when exposed to air or moisture for extended periods so it is crucial that you use very fresh malt extract. Once opened, store in an airtight container in the refrigerator to minimize moisture and slow the effects of aging.

Dried malt extract (DME)

A fine powder also known as spraymalt, DME is produced by heating sweet wort and spraying it inside a tall, heated unit. The droplets dry and quickly cool causing them to solidify and drop to the floor where they can be collected. To use DME, rehydrate it in a little cold water and then boil with hops to create a fermentable wort.

Liquid malt extract (LME)

This molasses-like substance is produced by heating sweet wort to evaporate some, but not all, of the liquid. Heating darkens the malt slightly, and this darkening will continue when it is boiled during brewing. If substituting LME for DME in a recipe, you will need 2½lb (1.2kg) of liquid malt extract for every 2¼lb (1kg) of dried.

Dried malt extract

Liquid malt extract

CANDI SUGAR
Often used in Belgian beers to increase the alcohol content without adding body, candi sugar is available in dark or light forms and adds depth of flavor.

HONEY
Most of the sugars in honey are fermentable, producing a dry yet distinctive honey character. Honey contains wild bacteria, so add near the end of the boil to sterilize.

MOLASSES
Also known simply as treacle, this dark, liquid sugar adds a complex, rumlike flavor. Use only in small quantities to add depth of character to high-alcohol ales.

MALTS, ADJUNCTS, AND SUGARS—AT A GLANCE

Name	Type	Description	Color (EBC)	Mash?	Max. usage
Acid malt	Malted grain	Lowers the mash pH of lagers; use in small quantities	3	✓	10%
Amber malt extract (dried and liquid)	Malt extract	Use in malt-extract recipes to add color	30	✗	100%
Amber malt	Malted grain	Imparts a deep amber color and biscuit flavors	65	✓	10%
Aromatic malt	Malted grain	Adds a rich malt character; similar to dark Munich malt	150	✓	10%
Barley hulls	Adjunct	Bulks up the mash and helps the runoff; provides no fermentable sugars	N/A	✗	10%
Biscuit malt	Malted grain	Adds biscuit character and color	50	✗	10%
Black malt	Malted grain	Adds flavor and color to dark beers; adds color to light beers	1,280	✗	10%
Bohemian Pilsner malt	Malted grain	Very light malt; requires multi-rest mashing (see p57)	2	✓	100%
Brewing sugar (dextrose)	Sugar	A highly fermentable sugar used to add dryness, aid fermentation, and reduce body in strong beers, such as double IPAs	2	✗	20%
Brown malt	Malted grain	Adds strong breadlike flavors; between amber and chocolate malt in color	105	✓	10%
Candi sugar (light and dark)	Sugar	Increases fermentable sugar levels; adds color and authentic flavors	N/A	✗	20%
Cara amber	Malted grain	Promotes a full body and adds a deep red color to amber and dark beers	70	✗	20%
Cara hell malt	Malted grain	Accentuates the fullness of the flavor in special German beers	25	✗	15%
Caramunich	Malted grain	Enhances flavor and aroma in golden to brown lagers and ales	200	✗	15%
Cara red	Malted grain	Adds body and increases the malt aroma in many beer styles	50	✗	10%
Cara rye malt	Malted grain	Introduces rye flavors and a pleasing brown color	150	✗	15%
Cara wheat malt	Malted grain	Promotes a full body, adds a wheat aroma, and enhances the color	100	✗	15%
Carafa special malt	Malted grain	Adds color and aroma to dark lagers; an alternative to black malt and roasted barley	800–1,500	✗	5%
Carapils	Malted grain	Very light crystal malt; adds body and malt flavor, without adding color	5	✗	20%
Chocolate malt	Malted grain	Adds color and aroma to dark beers; can also be used in pale ales	800	✗	10%
Corn sugar	Malted grain	Use to increase gravity without adding flavor or aroma	0	✗	5%
Crystal malt	Malted grain	Available in a range of colors; adds subtle caramel colors and flavors	60–400	✗	20%
Dark malt extract (dried and liquid)	Malt extract	Use to increase gravity and color	40	✗	100%
Extra light dried malt extract	Malt extract	The lightest malt extract; use for very low-color beers	5	✗	20%

Name	Type	Description	Color (EBC)	Mash?	Max. usage
Flaked barley	Adjunct	Adds a grainy flavor and improves head retention in stouts and porters	4	✓	20%
Flaked corn (maize)	Adjunct	Increases fermentable sugar level while adding very little flavor or color	2	✓	40%
Flaked oats	Adjunct	Used in small quantities in oatmeal stouts and New England IPAs	2	✓	10%
Flaked rice	Adjunct	Provides body without adding color or flavor	2	✓	20%
Honey	Sugar	Adds a dry finish with a distinct honey character	2	✗	100%
Lactose sugar	Sugar	A nonfermentable sugar made from milk, it is used to add sweetness and body to beers, such as sweet stouts and milkshake IPAs	2	✗	20%
Lager malt (or US domestic 2-row)	Malted grain	A light-colored base malt used for very pale beers	4	✓	100%
Light malt extract (dried and liquid)	Malted grain	A light malt extract used to increase the gravity in most malt-extract recipes	10	✗	100%
Low color pale	Malted grain	A very pale malt that is used in IPAs	4	✓	100%
Maple syrup	Sugar	Used to add a distinct, dry maple character	70	✗	10%
Melanoidin malt	Malted grain	Adds a full flavor and increases color and malt character	40	✓	15%
Mild ale malt	Malted grain	Use in brown ales and milds to impart extra flavor	10	✓	100%
Munich malt	Malted grain	Similar to Vienna malt, but slightly more roasted; adds lots of malt character	20	✓	50%
Pale malt	Malted grain	A base malt used in the majority of ales	5	✓	100%
Peat-smoked malt	Malted grain	A heavily smoked malt	3	✓	20%
Pilsner malt	Malted grain	Similar to lager malt but usually produced using two-row barley (see p20)	3	✓	100%
Roasted barley	Adjunct	Adds nutty, roasted flavors and a deep red-to-brown color	1,000	✗	10%
Roasted wheat	Adjunct	Adds a deep brown color to dark wheat beers	900	✓	10%
Rye malt	Malted grain	Use to add rye flavors and spicy notes	10	✓	50%
Smoked malt	Malted grain	Usually smoked over beech; adds a distinctive smoky aroma to smoked beers	18	✓	100%
Special B malt	Malted grain	Adds a deep caramel color and flavor	250	✓	10%
Spelt malt	Malted grain	Imparts spelt aroma notes	5	✓	20%
Torrified wheat	Adjunct	Use in wheat beers, and to aid head retention and flavor in ales	4	✓	40%
Victory malt	Malted grain	Adds an orange color and nutty flavors	50	✓	15%
Vienna malt	Malted grain	Use in light amber beers for color and flavor	8	✓	50%
Wheat malt extract (dried and liquid)	Malt extract	Use in malt-extract wheat beers, and to aid head retention in other beer styles	16	✗	100%

HOPS

Hops are the cone-shaped flowers of the female hop plant—a climbing bine related to hemp. They are dried and added to beer for bitterness, flavor, and aroma and to protect it from bacteria.

Native to North America, Europe, and Asia, hops are first thought to have been used in beer production in the 11th century. They were used instead of bitter herbs—such as dandelion, marigold, and heather— since they produced beer that was less likely to spoil.

Today, due to extensive breeding programs aimed at creating more productive and disease-resistant plants, more than 100 different varieties are grown around the world. The main growing regions are the US, New Zealand, the UK, Germany, the Czech Republic, China, Poland, and Australia.

GROWING AND HARVESTING

Hop plants, which grow best vertically, are trained to grow up stringed supports—they can reach heights of up to 20ft (6m). The string supports are lowered during harvesting, allowing the cones from the tallest bines to be removed easily. Smaller dwarf varieties are also propagated, although these need to be grown over a larger area to yield a comparable crop.

Traditionally, hops were harvested by hand. Due to the high numbers of people required at harvest time, hop picking became something of a social event. In England, for example, whole families would travel from towns and cities to the hop-growing regions on specially chartered trains and buses, living in temporary huts and spending several weeks picking the hop harvest. Today, hops are picked and dried mechanically, although the hop harvest is still a time of excitement, with many breweries producing beers made using undried "green" hops to celebrate the new harvest.

Fresh hop cones

Hop bines are trained to grow vertically up stringed supports, which can be lowered during harvesting.

BITTERING AND AROMA HOPS

Hops are added at various intervals during the boil (see p59) to impart particular characteristics to the finished beer. Hops added at the start of the boil impart bitterness, which balances the alcohol flavors and adds smoothness to the beer. Hops added later in the boil—typically during the final 30 minutes—impart flavor and aroma. These tend to be added in several additions depending on the desired character.

Another way of importing aroma and flavor from hops is to use a traditional method known as first-wort hopping, in which hops are added to the runoff from the mash (see p57) before the boil. The hops are steeped, which causes them to oxidize and allows some of the beta acids to dissolve into the wort rather than being driven off. In blind tests, beers produced using this method were found to have a smoother bitterness and aroma, so it's worth experimenting.

Historically, hops were categorized as either bittering hops or aroma hops. Today, however, increasing numbers of hop varieties are suitable for both bittering and aroma and are known as dual-purpose hops.

ALPHA AND BETA ACIDS

Hop resins contain alpha and beta acids, which have key roles in the brewing process:

Alpha acids impart a bitter flavor and possess antibacterial properties. The level of alpha acids in a hop variety is measured as a percentage—the higher the figure, the higher the levels of bitterness that can be potentially extracted. Alpha acids are not soluble in water and therefore require boiling. The longer the boil time, the more alpha acids that will be dissolved and the greater the final bitterness.

Beta acids impart aroma to a beer and do not require boiling. They contain highly volatile essential oils, which are driven off by the steam of the boil, so it is best to add them in the final minutes of the boil or once the boil is complete. These delicate acids can also be added during fermentation, a process known as dry hopping.

KEEPING HOPS FRESH

Dried hops react with light and air and so deteriorate relatively quickly. For this reason, they are usually supplied in light-protective, vacuum-sealed packets. You can store hops in unopened packets for about two years, but once opened and exposed to the air, they will quickly dry out and lose their delicate essential oils. As they are usually packed in 3½oz (100g) quantities, and many beers require several different varieties, you may end up with lots of half-used packs. To keep them fresh, simply seal and store in the freezer, using direct from frozen when required.

Add dried hops at various stages of the boil, depending on whether they are intended for bitterness, flavor, or aroma.

HOPS FOR BREWING

Fresh hops must be air-dried before they can be used in brewing. This helps preserve them and locks in the flavors and aromas. The recipes in this book call for dried whole-leaf hops, which have the most natural flavor, although they can deteriorate quickly if exposed to air. Processed hop pellets are a popular alternative and have a longer shelf life.

Dried whole-leaf hops

Hop pellets

HOPS—AT A GLANCE

Hop name	Country of origin	Alpha acid range	Character description	Flavor intensity (1 = low; 10 = high)
Admiral	UK	14–16%	Resinous, citrus, orange	9
Ahtanum	US	5–8%	Floral, citrus, lemon	7
Amarillo	US	7–11%	Floral, citrus, orange	9
Apollo	US	15–19%	Resinous, strong herbal	8
Atlas	Slovenia	5–9%	Lime, floral, pine	6
Aurora	Slovenia	5–9%	Lime, floral, pine	6
Azzaca	US	11–14%	Orange, papaya, lemon	8
Bobek (Styrian Golding)	Slovenia	2–5%	Pine, lemon, floral	8
Bramling Cross	UK	5–8%	Spicy, black currant	8
Brewer's Gold	Germany	5–9%	Spicy, black currant, lemon	8
Cascade	US/UK/NZ	5–9%	Lychee, floral, grapefruit	9
Celia (Styrian Golding)	Slovenia	2–5%	Lemon, pine, floral	8
Centennial	US	7–12%	Lemon, herbal, resinous	9
Challenger	UK	5–9%	Spicy, cedar, green tea	7
Chinook	US	11–15%	Grapefruit, citrus, pine	9
Citra	US	11–14%	Mango, tropical fruit, lime	9
Cluster	US	6–9%	Blackberry, spicy	6
Columbus	US	14–20%	Sherbert, black pepper, licorice	9
Crystal	US	3–6%	Tangerine, citrus	6
Delta	US	4–7%	Pineapple, pear	5
East Kent Golding	UK	5–8%	Spicy, honey, earthy	6
Ekuanot	US	13–15%	Citrus, tropical fruit, herbal	8
First Gold	UK	6–9%	Orange, marmalade, spicy	6
Fuggle	UK	4–7%	Grassy, minty, earthy	6
Galaxy	Australia	13–15%	Passion fruit, peaches	8
Galena	US	10–14%	Black currant, spicy, grapefruit	6
Golding	UK	4–8%	Spicy, honey, earthy	6
Green Bullet	NZ	10–13%	Pine, raisin, black pepper	7
Hersbrucker	Germany	2–4%	Floral, herbal	6
Liberty	US	3–5%	Spicy, lemon, citrus	6
Manderina Bavaria	Germany	7–10%	Fruity, citrus	6
Mittlefrüh	Germany	3–6%	Herbal, floral, grassy	6

Hop name	Country of origin	Alpha acid range	Character description	Flavor intensity (1 = low; 10 = high)
Mosaic	US	10–14%	Mango, citrus, pine	8
Motueka	NZ	5–8%	Lemon, lime, floral	8
Mount Hood	US	4–7%	Herbal, grapefruit	6
Nelson Sauvin	NZ	10–13%	Gooseberry, grapefruit	9
Newport	US	13–17%	Cedar, estery, herbal	7
Northdown	UK	6–9%	Spicy, cedar, pine	7
Northern Brewer	Germany	5–9%	Spicy, resinous, herbal	6
Nugget	US	10–14%	Spicy, pear, peach	6
Pacific Gem	NZ	13–18%	Blackberry, oak, pine	7
Pacific Jade	NZ	12–14%	Herbal, lemon zest, black pepper	8
Pacifica	NZ	4–8%	Herbal, orange, citrus	6
Palisade	US	6–10%	Citrus, black currant, grapefruit	7
Perle	Germany	6–9%	Spicy, cedar, orange	7
Pilgrim	UK	9–12%	Spicy, cedar, honey	6
Pioneer	UK	9–12%	Cedar, grapefruit, herbal	8
Pride of Ringwood	Australia	9–12%	Cedar, oak, herbal	5
Progress	UK	5–8%	Spicy, honey, grassy	6
Riwaka	NZ	5–8%	Grapefruit, lime, tropical fruit	8
Saaz	Czech Republic	2–5%	Earthy, herbal, floral	5
Santiam	US	4–7%	Herbal, peach, lemon	6
Savinski (Styrian Golding)	Slovenia	2–4%	Lemon, lime, earthy	8
Simcoe	US	11–15%	Pine, grapefruit, passion fruit	6
Sorachi Ace	US	10–14%	Lemon, coconut	7
Sovereign	UK	4–7%	Grassy, floral, earthy	6
Spalt Select	Germany	2–5%	Herbal, floral, earthy	5
Summer	Australia	4–7%	Apricot, melon	6
Summit	US	13–15%	Pink grapefruit, orange	9
Target	UK	9–12%	Pine, cedar, licorice	9
Tettnang	Germany	4–7%	Earthy, herbal, floral	5
Vic Secret	Australia	14–17%	Pineapple, herbal	7
Wai-ti	NZ	2–4%	Mandarin, lemon, lime zest	6
Wakatu	NZ	7–10%	Vanilla, floral, lime	7
Warrior	US	13–15%	Resinous, herbal, pine	6
WGV	UK	5–8%	Spicy, herbal, earthy	7
Willamette	US	4–7%	Black currant, spicy, floral	6

YEAST

Yeast is the ingredient that turns the sweet wort produced from malt, hops, and water into beer. It is a single-celled life form and type of fungus.

Yeast has been used to create beer for thousands of years, but it wasn't until the development of the microscope in the 17th century that its existence was first noted. Prior to this, brewers had simply left their wort uncovered, with fermentation taking place thanks to wild yeast spores in the atmosphere. Then, in 1857, the French chemist and microbiologist Louis Pasteur proved the importance of yeast in fermentation. Pasteur's discovery changed the way beer was produced, allowing brewers to gain greater control over the fermentation process.

YEAST AND BREWING

There are thought to be more than 1,500 different species of yeast in existence, but only two are used for the majority of beers—*Saccharomyces cerevisiae* (more often used to make ale) and *Saccharomyces pastorianus* (more often lager). Some beers use a third species—*Brettanomyces* (see box, below). When added to wort,

the yeast cells feed on the sugars and carbohydrates contained in the sweet liquid, and produce carbon dioxide and ethanol (alcohol) as a result. The yeast also produces several by-products that affect the flavor and aroma of the finished beer. The most common by-products are esters, fusel alcohols, and diacetyl:

■ Esters are chemical compounds that contribute important flavor characteristics—typically complex fruit characters. They are found in varying amounts in many types of beers, especially ales and Belgian-style beers. The amount of esters produced depends in part on the fermentation temperature—the higher the temperature, the more esters produced.

■ Fusel alcohols are a mixture of various alcohol compounds, and they create hot, spicy, notes in the finished beer. Although they can be found in many beer styles, if they become too noticeable, they are generally considered to be a flaw. In fact, the word "fusel" is German for "bad liquor."

■ Like fusel alcohols, the presence of too much diacetyl is seen as a flaw in most beer styles, particularly lagers. Although it may exist in small, discreet amounts in many beers, in larger quantities it can deliver overpowering butter and butterscotch flavors and aromas. Diacetyl is usually "cleaned up" by the yeast once fermentation is complete, so its presence in the finished beer is often a sign of poor fermentation.

TOP- AND BOTTOM-FERMENTING YEASTS

The two main species of yeasts used in brewing can be distinguished by how they ferment. *S. cerevisiae* is top-fermenting, while *S. pastorianus* is bottom-fermenting.

Many Belgian beers are brewed with Brett, which imparts complex fruit flavors during fermentation (see right).

BRETTANOMYCES YEAST

Brett beer is made with a wild yeast called *Brettanomyces* (Brett). This yeast creates wonderful, complex flavors and aromas and is often used in conjunction with souring bacteria (see pp66–67).

As a yeast, Brett can be used as a primary fermenter instead of *Saccharomyces* (see left) and will ferment the wort to completion, producing both CO2 and alcohol. Brett ferments beer more slowly than *Saccharomyces* and so requires larger pitch rates if used in primary fermentation.

Top-fermenting yeasts work best at higher fermentation temperatures, typically 60–75°F (16–24°C) and are so called because they rise to the top of the fermenter during fermentation. These yeasts produce lots of complex esters, especially at higher temperatures, which results in a wide range of flavors and aromas. Top-fermenting yeasts are subdivided into ale and wheat strains due to their distinct flavor characteristics.

Bottom-fermenting yeasts, on the other hand, work best at lower fermentation temperatures, typically 45–60°F (7–15°C), and settle out at the bottom of the fermenter. These yeasts tend to result in beers with a clean, neutral flavor. Due to the lower fermentation temperatures, they produce fewer esters but more diacetyl than top-fermenting yeasts. Many bottom-fermenting yeasts require a "diacetyl rest" (during which the temperature is raised for a few days at the end of fermentation), which helps reduce the levels of diacetyl.

FLOCCULATION AND ATTENUATION

All yeasts can be measured in terms of their flocculation and attenuation rates. Flocculation is a measure of how easily the yeast falls out of suspension in the wort, which affects how quickly and easily the beer will clear—the higher the flocculation rate, the quicker the beer will clear. Highly flocculating yeasts may need to be roused, or stirred, during fermentation to lift the particles back into suspension and so allow fermentation to complete successfully.

Attenuation is a measure of how efficiently the yeast will ferment the available sugars. It is usually measured as a percentage, with, for example, a 100 percent attenuation rate indicating that a yeast will ferment all the sugars in the wort to alcohol. Yeasts that have high attenuation rates generally have low flocculation rates, and vice versa.

REUSING YEAST

Although some yeasts—typically those in liquid form (see below)—are expensive, you can reuse them. Simply collect about 17½fl oz (500ml) of sediment from the bottom of the fermenter after fermentation is complete and store it in a sterilized container in the fridge. If used within a couple of weeks, you can pitch this yeast directly into your next batch of wort. Don't worry if you leave it longer than two weeks, though, as you can still reuse yeast by making a starter (see pp60–61). Alternatively, time your brew days so that the sediment from one batch can be pitched into the wort of a new batch.

Liquid yeasts can be reused three or four times; dried yeasts are not suitable for reuse, but they are relatively inexpensive.

If using liquid yeast, you will first need to make a yeast starter to increase the number of active cells.

Forms of yeasts

Yeasts for home brewing are available dried and in fresh liquid form. Dried yeast has a long shelf life and is easy to use, but the range can be limited. The main brands are Fermentis and Danstar. In contrast, there are many liquid yeasts available, allowing you to brew any beer you choose. Liquid yeast does, however, have a short shelf life, and you will need to make a starter (see pp60–61). Wyeast and White Labs are the main brands.

Dried yeast

Fresh liquid yeast

YEASTS—AT A GLANCE

The availability of fresh yeast can vary, so use this chart to find
alternative yeasts for some of the key recipes in the book (note
that not all recipes can be accurately produced using dried yeast).

Beer style	Beer name	Liquid yeast		Dried yeast
		Option 1	Option 2	
Light Lager	European Lager (see p76)	Wyeast 2007 Pilsen Lager	White Labs 830 German Lager	Fermentis 34/70
Light Lager	Dortmunder Export (see pp78–79)	Wyeast 2124 Bohemian Lager	White Labs 830 German Lager	Fermentis S23
Light Lager	Japanese Rice Lager (see p81)	Wyeast 2278 Czech Pils	White Labs 800 Pilsner	Fermentis 34/70
Pilsner	Czech Pilsner (see pp82–83)	Wyeast 2001 Urquell	White Labs 800 Pilsner	Fermentis 34/70
Pilsner	German Pilsner (see p85)	Wyeast 2007 Pilsen Lager	White Labs 840 American Lager	Fermentis 34/70
Pilsner	American Pilsner (see p87)	Wyeast 2124 Bohemian Lager	White Labs 840 American Lager	Fermentis 34/70
Amber Lager	Vienna Lager (see pp88–89)	Wyeast 2124 Bohemian Lager	White Labs 830 German Lager	Fermentis 34/70
Amber Lager	Oktoberfest (see p90)	Wyeast 2206 Bavarian Lager	White Labs 820 Oktoberfest	Fermentis 34/70
Bock	Helles Bock (see p91)	Wyeast 2487 Hella Bock	White Labs 833 German Bock	Fermentis 34/70
Bock	Doppelbock (see p94)	Wyeast 2124 Bohemian Lager	White Labs 830 German Lager	Fermentis 34/70
Bock	Eisbock (see p95)	Wyeast 2308 Munich Lager	White Labs 838 Southern German Lager	Fermentis 34/70
Dark Lager	Munich Dunkel (see p98)	Wyeast 2278 Czech Pils	White Labs 830 German Lager	Fermentis 34/70
Dark Lager	Black Lager (see p99)	White Labs WLP850 Copenhagen Lager	White Labs WLP802 Czech Lager	Fermentis S23
Pale Ale	Spring Beer (see p104)	Wyeast 1275 Thames Valley Ale	White Labs 023 Burton Ale	Danstar Nottingham
Pale Ale	Harvest Pale Ale (see p106)	Wyeast 1272 American Ale II	White Labs 060 American Ale Yeast Blend	Fermentis US05
Pale Ale	ESB Ale (see p107)	Wyeast 1187 Ringwood Ale	White Labs 005 British Ale	Fermentis S04
Pale Ale	Pale Ale (see pp110–111)	Wyeast 1187 Ringwood Ale	White Labs 005 British Ale	Danstar Nottingham
Pale Ale	Honey Ale (see p112)	Wyeast 1098 British Ale	White Labs 007 Dry English Ale	Danstar Nottingham
Pale Ale	Kveik Farmhouse Ale (see pp116–117)	Yeast Bay Sigmund's Voss Kveik	Omega Labs Hornindal Kveik	N/A
Pale Ale	Double Dry Hopped Pale Ale (see p120)	Wyeast 1318 London Ale III	White Labs 007 Dry English Ale	Fermentis S04

Beer style	Beer Name	Liquid yeast		Dried Yeast
		Option 1	Option 2	
IPA	Brett IPA (see pp128–129)	Yeast Bay WLP4637—Amalgamation—Brett Super Blend	Omega Labs BRING ON DA FUNK	N/A
IPA	English IPA (see p121)	Wyeast 1187 Ringwood	White Labs 005 British Ale	Fermentis US05
IPA	American IPA (see p125)	Wyeast 1272 American Ale II	White Labs 060 American Ale Yeast Blend	Fermentis US05
IPA	Black IPA (see p127)	Wyeast 1187 Ringwood Ale	White Labs 005 British Ale	Fermentis US05
Bitter	London Bitter (see p140)	Wyeast 1318 London Ale III	White Labs 013 London Ale	Fermentis S04
Bitter	Irish Red Ale (see p145)	Wyeast 1084 Irish Ale	White Labs 004 Irish Ale	Fermentis S33
Strong Ale	Bière de Garde (see pp148–149)	Wyeast 3711 French Saison	White Labs 566 Saison II	N/A
Strong Ale	Winter Warmer (see p150)	Wyeast 1968 London ESB Ale	White Labs 002 English Ale	Fermentis S04
Strong Ale	Belgian Blonde Ale (see p154)	Wyeast 1388 Belgian Strong Ale	White Labs 570 Belgian Golden Ale	N/A
Strong Ale	Belgian Dubbel (see p155)	Wyeast 3944 Belgian Witbier	White Labs 400 Belgian Wit Ale	Fermentis WB06
Brown Ale	Southern Brown Ale (see p161)	Wyeast 1187 Ringwood Ale	White Labs 005 British Ale	Fermentis US05
Mild	Mild (see p164)	Wyeast 1318 London Ale III	White Labs 013 London	Fermentis US05
Barley Wine	English Barley Wine (see pp166–167)	Wyeast 1028 London Ale	White Labs 013 London	Fermentis S33
Barley Wine	American Barley Wine (see p168)	Wyeast 1056 American Ale	White Labs 001 California Ale	Fermentis S33
Stout	Dry Stout (see p174)	Wyeast 1084 Irish Ale	White Labs 004 Irish Ale	Fermentis US05
Porter	Brown Porter (see p169)	Wyeast 1028 London Ale	White Labs 013 London Ale	Fermentis US05
Weissbier	Weizenbock (see p186)	Wyeast 3056 Bavarian Wheat Blend	White Labs 380 Hefeweizen IV	Danstar Munich
Rye Beer	Roggenbier (see p192)	Wyeast 3638 Bavarian Wheat	White Labs 380 Hefeweizen IV	Fermentis WB06
Witbier	Witbier (see pp194–195)	Wyeast 3944 Belgian Witbier	White Labs 400 Belgian Wit Ale	Fermentis WB06
Dark Wheat Beer	Dunkelweizen (see p196)	Wyeast 3056 Bavarian Wheat Blend	White Labs 380 Hefeweizen IV	Fermentis WB06
Light hybrid	Kölsch (see p201)	Wyeast 2565 Kölsch	White Labs 029 German Ale	Fermentis US05
Amber hybrid	Californian Common (see p202)	Wyeast 2112 California Ale	White Labs 810 San Francisco Lager	Fermentis US05

BREWING **LIQUOR**

Water—known as liquor by brewers—is the main ingredient
in beer. As a result, the quality and chemical profile of the water
you use can have a noticeable effect on the finished beer.

The chemical makeup of your water supply depends on
the journey it takes to reach your tap. As rainwater (all
of our water starts off as rainwater) precipitates through
the ground, it can pick up various minerals, depending on
the type of rock it passes through. Some minerals, such
as calcium and magnesium, are soluble in water.
Known as ions, these soluble minerals are absorbed
into the water supply. Water with a high mineral content
is classified as hard, while water with a low mineral
content—typically water that passes through rock such
as slate or granite—is classified as soft.

BEER STYLES AND WATER
Before chemical analysis of water was available, beer
styles were often dictated by the chemical makeup
of the local water supply. If you want to reproduce a
certain style of beer, replicating the water from that

region will help you achieve authentic results. For
example, the water profile of the Pilsen region of the
Czech Republic—the home of Pilsner lagers—has some
of the softest water in the world, with almost no
mineral content. This results in exceptionally clear,
clean-tasting lagers. By contrast, Dublin in Ireland—
the home of Guinness, the famous dry stout—has very
hard water containing high levels of bicarbonates and
calcium. This gives the water a high pH, which is then
balanced out by the acidity of the highly roasted malts
to create the perfect stout.

KIT AND MALT-EXTRACT BREWING
For kit and malt-extract brewing (see pp52–55), the
chemical makeup of your water will have only a minor
effect on the finished beer—if the water tastes and
smells good, it should produce good beer. The only

Soft water is great for producing light lagers
with a crisp, clean taste

The best stouts are brewed using
hard water, which has a high pH

potential cause for concern is if your water supplier adds high levels of chlorine or chloramine, as these antibacterial chemicals can react with the yeast and create unwanted medicinal flavors (see below for simple water treatments).

FULL-MASH BREWING

For full-mash brewing (see pp56–59), the chemical makeup of your water becomes much more important. Specifically, during the mash (see p57), the acidity of your water and the makeup of your grain bill will determine the pH of your mash. If the pH is not between 5.2 and 5.8, the enzymes (and their ability to convert the starch in the malts) will be negatively affected.

Later, during fermentation, the pH levels will naturally drop as the yeast ferments the sugars in the wort. This has the benefit of creating a more unfriendly environment for unwanted bacteria. Getting the pH levels right can also help with the clarity and overall quality of the finished beer.

If your water supply has high levels of chlorine, boil it for about 30 minutes before use

WATER ANALYSIS

Digital pH tester

In brewing terms, the important ions in water are calcium, magnesium, bicarbonate, sodium, chloride, and sulfate. Your water company should be able to provide a report that gives a chemical breakdown of the local water supply. You can then add calcium sulphate (gypsum), magnesium sulphate, or sodium to alter these levels as necessary—to adjust the pH levels required for a specific recipe. Working out these additions and adjustments can be complicated, but there are several calculators online that will make the various calculations for you (see p219 for more information).

TESTING THE MASH

Simply use a pH strip or digital pH reader to measure the mash pH, then record the results so you can adjust the water for the next brew. It is worth remembering, however, that while it is useful to know the profile of your water profile in full-mash brewing, when emulating a certain beer style, you can still make great beer without adjusting your water's pH and mineral levels.

SIMPLE WATER TREATMENTS

If, for example, your water is hard and you want to brew a full-mash lager or Pilsner recipe that requires soft

water, you could simply mix your tap water with a large proportion of distilled or deionized water, which is available to buy. This will help maintain the correct mash pH and avoid astringent tannin flavors being introduced to the finished beer.

To remove chlorine, you can either leave the water you will need for brewing to stand overnight, or you can boil it for 30 minutes before use. Chloramine, however, cannot be removed by boiling. The easiest way to remove both chlorine and chloramine is to add a crushed Campden tablet to your water a few minutes before using.

For kit and malt-extract brewers, the most important consideration is that your water is free from chlorine and chloramine—and if you are lucky enough to have great-tasting water straight from the tap, there is no need to treat it at all.

BREWER'S TIP

An alternative to treating your own tap water is to use bottled mineral water. Although this is more expensive, bottled water is convenient and ideal for brewing.

HERBS, FLOWERS, FRUITS, AND SPICES

Originally used in place of hops to add flavor and protect the beer from bacteria, you can use any of these ingredients to introduce a range of fascinating flavors and aromas.

COCONUT
Works really well in a variety of beer styles, but probably best in dark stout or porter styles. Use toasted chips and add at the end of fermentation.

CARDAMOM SEEDS
Popular in Belgian-style beers, cardamom complements coriander, cumin, and citrus flavors. Add in the last few minutes of the boil or about four days into fermentation.

CORIANDER SEEDS
This works well alongside bitter orange in witbiers, imparting a distinctive flavor. Add in the last few minutes of the boil or about four days into fermentation.

STAR ANISE
Use star anise in Belgian-style ales and festive brews to add a pungent, sweet flavor. Add in the last few minutes of the boil or about four days into fermentation.

CINNAMON STICKS
Cinnamon imparts a distinctively festive aroma and flavor, so use it in dark, full-bodied beers. Add in the last few minutes of the boil or about four days into fermentation.

LICORICE ROOT
This imparts a distinctive, sweet flavor for use in strong festive and vintage beers. Add in the last few minutes of the boil or about four days into fermentation.

VANILLA BEANS
Use just one or two vanilla beans in stout and porter recipes to add a sweet, warm flavor. Add in the last few minutes of the boil or about four days into fermentation.

CHILE PEPPERS
Use in Mexican beers and light lagers to add a subtle, dry aftertaste and a slight burn; also great for novelty beers. Add about four days into fermentation.

JUNIPER BERRIES
The main flavoring in gin, you can also add juniper to beers for a subtle ginlike flavor. Add in the last few minutes of the boil or about four days into fermentation.

ROSE HIPS
Use rose hips sparingly to lend character to festive and strong beers. Add in the last few minutes of the boil or about four days into fermentation.

BLUEBERRIES
These work well in many styles, adding both flavor and color. Can be quite subtle, so you may need more than you think. Add at the end of fermentation.

PEACHES
A subtle flavor that works well in lots of different styles. Try it in beers that contain citrusy hops. Add at the end of fermentation.

APRICOTS
These are best suited to sour beers, as the sweetness really complements the acidity. Add apricots at the end of fermentation.

ELDERBERRIES

Often used in wine, elderberries introduce a portlike flavor that works well in strong festive beers. Add a small amount about four days into fermentation.

ELDERFLOWERS

Great in summer ales but can be overpowering so use in small amounts. Add in the last few minutes of the boil or about four days into fermentation.

KAFFIR LIME LEAVES

With a spicy flavor and aroma, kaffir lime leaves introduce a clean, citrus flavor. Add in the last minutes of the boil or about four days into fermentation.

STRAWBERRIES

Use a few strawberries in pale beers and lagers for a subtle sweetness. Add about four days into fermentation.

RASPBERRIES

Work well in Belgian wheat and sour beers to impart a sweet, fruity character. Add approximately four days into fermentation.

CHERRIES

Popular in Belgian-style Kriek beers, cherries balance the alcohol and bitterness. Add about four days into fermentation.

ORANGE PEEL

Use orange peel in strong Belgian and festive beers. Bitter orange peel (or Curaçao) adds zesty orange flavors to Belgian and wheat beers but, despite the name, no bitterness. Add in the last few minutes of the boil or about four days into fermentation.

LEMON AND LIME PEEL

Lemon peel works well in pale ales and light summer beers, adding a zesty, citrus character. Lime peel also works well in pale ales, complementing coriander and lemongrass and gives a refreshing zing. Add in the last few minutes of the boil or about four days into fermentation.

HEATHER TIPS

Traditionally used in Scottish ales known as Fraoch, heather imparts a grassy, minty aroma and flavor. Traditionally, heather tips were used instead of hops due to their bittering qualities. Add in the last few minutes of the boil or about four days into fermentation.

TEA

Great in IPAs and sour beers, the aroma and flavor vary with tea variety. Lightly steam to sterilize and release aroma, then add at the end of fermentation.

COFFEE

Coffee tastes great in a wide variety of different beer styles, from pale ales to stouts. Best to add lightly crushed beans at the end of fermentation.

NUTS

Use in dark beers. Nuts must be roasted to minimize oil, which can damage head retention. Almonds and peanuts both work well. Add at the end of fermentation.

GETTING
STARTED

BEFORE YOU BEGIN

Brewing your own beer should be an enjoyable and rewarding
experience. To make sure the process runs smoothly, there are
four key factors to consider before you begin.

WHAT STYLE OF BEER DO YOU WANT TO BREW?
You should be able to re-create at home any style of
beer available commercially. However, due to the
processes involved, some styles require additional
equipment and more advanced techniques. If you
are new to brewing, start with a relatively simple
recipe such as a pale ale (see pp104–120), bitter (see
pp140–147), or stout (see pp174–183). Lager recipes
(see pp74–99) are usually more complicated to produce
as they need to be fermented and stored at cooler
temperatures. If you do decide to brew a lager,
acquiring an old fridge and connecting it to a digital
temperature controller (see p51) will allow you to
regulate the temperature for the best results.

TIPS FOR SUCCESSFUL HOME BREWING

• Make sure you have the required equipment and ingredients
before you start.
Create a checklist so you know what to do at every stage.

• Order extra packets of dried yeast, malt extract, and
brewing sugar—this could prevent a whole batch of beer
from going to waste should the yeast fail, for example, or if
extra sugar is required.

• Start early, since brew days can take longer than
anticipated, especially when using the full-mash method.

• Consider teaming up with a friend—it's more fun, and you
can split the costs and share the workload.

• Avoid sampling previous batches of beer until you've
finished brewing for the day!

Start off with an ale or bitter recipe,
as they are quick and easy

Lagers require more skill and equipment
than most ale recipes

WHICH METHOD ARE YOU GOING TO USE?

There are three main ways to produce beer at home—using a kit, malt extract, or the full-mash method (see pp56–59). The method you choose will determine the type of equipment and ingredients you will need to buy before you start.

The simplest way to make beer is from a kit. These are great for beginners as they are simple to use and produce high-quality beer. Don't worry if you move on to more advanced methods—the equipment needed for making beer with a kit is also required for malt-extract and full-mash brewing, so your investment won't be wasted.

The malt-extract method is also straightforward and will allow you to brew a wider range of beers. Many of the recipes in this book feature malt-extract variations.

Kits are quick, easy, and can produce professional-tasting beer

WHERE ARE YOU GOING TO BREW?

Brewing can be a messy job so choosing the right room in the house in which to make your beer is an important decision. For most people, the kitchen is the best place to prepare the wort, as there is easy access to fresh water, drainage, and a heat source. Alternatively, as lots of strong-smelling steam will be created when boiling malt-extract and full-mash recipes, an outside space may be preferable.

Once you have created a wort, you will need to find a suitable place to leave 6 gallons (23 liters) of liquid to ferment at a constant temperature and away from direct sunlight. Most ale yeasts, for example, require a warm ambient temperature, so you may need a heater (see p48) if brewing in a cold place.

You may decide to simply boil the wort on an ordinary kitchen stove top

FIND A GOOD SUPPLIER

As you experiment with brewing your own beer, you will need equipment, ingredients, and perhaps some friendly advice—so finding a good supplier is key. If you are lucky enough to have a specialty supplier locally, pay them a visit. Most will be more than happy to offer advice. Look for a supplier with a good range of yeasts (including liquid varieties), vacuum-packed hops, and equipment.

If you don't have a home-brew store in your area, there are several online retailers who will be able to supply equipment and ingredients. They should be able to provide advice and support if needed. Online forums are also a great way to pick up tips and share your experiences with other home brewers.

With a wide range of ingredients, you can experiment with different beer styles

THREE METHODS OF BREWING

Brewing beer at home can be as easy or involved as you wish. There are three main ways of making up a wort—each method more advanced than the last.

METHOD 1—USING A KIT

Brewing using a kit (see pp52–53 for step-by-step techniques) is the simplest way to make beer at home. A wort is prepared in advance by a malt producer, who then removes most of the water to create a small volume of concentrated, molasses-like liquid. This is rehydrated by the home brewer to make up the volume for a full batch of beer. It takes only 20–30 minutes and requires no prior knowledge. The quality of home-brew kits has improved greatly in recent years, with professional breweries developing kits that closely replicate their commercial beers.

ADVANTAGES	DISADVANTAGES
• Quick to prepare • Simple to use and requires no prior knowledge • Requires only basic equipment	• Offers little scope to customize a recipe • Any hop aroma is likely to have been lost during the production process

METHOD 2—USING MALT EXTRACT

Brewing with malt extract (see pp54–55 for step-by-step techniques) involves adding unhopped malt extract—either in liquid or dried form—to water and boiling it with hops, which are added at various intervals. The wort is then cooled to produce a fermentable wort. This method is more involved than using a kit and requires additional equipment (see pp46–51), but you will be rewarded for the effort as malt-extract brewing is highly regarded in brewing circles and can produce award-winning beers.

ADVANTAGES	DISADVANTAGES
• A variety of beers and styles can be produced • Specialty grains can be used for flavor • You are more involved in the process so will gain confidence and knowledge	• Not all malts are available in extract form • It is the most expensive method, due to the high cost of malt extract • Requires additional time and equipment

METHOD 3—FULL-MASH BREWING

The full-mash method, also known as all-grain brewing, is the technique used in professional breweries. It consists of three key processes—the mash, sparge, and boil (see pp56–59 for step-by-step techniques). Full-mash brewing offers maximum flexibility and allows you to replicate any style of beer. It does, however, require the most knowledge, equipment, time, and effort and so is not suitable for everyone. Typically, a home brewer advances through the first two methods, gaining experience and confidence, before moving on to full-mash brewing.

ADVANTAGES	DISADVANTAGES
• No limit to the number of styles that can be produced	• Requires the most amount of equipment
• The cheapest way to produce beer	• A brew day can last several hours
• Offers complete control over ingredients used	• Can generate a lot of mess
• Produces the highest quality beer	• More things can go wrong!

Three-tiered brewing setup

Full-mash brewers typically use three separate vessels—a hot liquor tank or HLT for heating and storing all the water (known as liquor by brewers), a mash tun for mixing malted grain with hot water to produce a sweet wort, and a boiler for boiling the wort with hops to sterilize it and add flavor and aroma. In a home environment, the flow of water and wort is usually achieved via gravity using a tiered setup. Side-by-side systems can also be used, but a pump would be required.

Hot liquor tank (HLT)

Mash tun

Boiler

Brew-in-a-bag method

Full-mash brews can also be produced in a single boiling vessel, known as the brew in a bag or BIAB method. All the water is heated to mash temperature in a boiler, grains are added in a bag for the mash, and then the bag is removed before the boil. The set-up costs are cheaper and the process is quicker and less messy than a typical full-mash brew, but you will need a very large boiling vessel and the mashing process is less efficient.

There are now many all-in-one brewing systems that operate on this basis. Although relatively expensive, they reduce the difficulty of full-mash brewing by automating much of the process. Another advantage is that you need to clean and store only a single piece of equipment.

THE **IMPORTANCE** OF **SANITATION**

The key to producing great beer is to pay proper attention to sanitation.
In fact, commercial brewers spend as much time cleaning and sterilizing
equipment as they do brewing beer.

Poor sanitation is the biggest cause of spoiled batches
of beer. While prepared wort is the ideal environment
for propagating yeast cells, it is also the perfect host for
other unfriendly, wild yeast and bacteria—and once a
beer has become contaminated, it usually cannot be
saved. Good sanitation is particularly important during
the warmer summer months, when there is a greater
risk from airborne bacteria.

CLEANING AND STERILIZING

Good sanitation means thoroughly cleaning and
sterilizing all your brewing equipment. Get into the
habit of cleaning equipment immediately after use—
dirt and debris is much easier to remove before it has
had a chance to dry. Also, remember to remove the taps
from your vessels and carefully scrub the threads, as
this is a common problem area.

Once cleaned, equipment must be sterilized to kill off
any bacteria. Every piece of equipment that comes into
contact with the wort after the boil must be sterilized,
including trial jars, hydrometers, thermometers, and
spoons. Depending on the type of sterilizer you decide
to use (see opposite), you may have to rinse it off
afterward.

For
convenience,
sterilize small
pieces of
equipment inside
the fermenter

CLEANING BOTTLES

This can be an arduous task, especially if yeast sediment has
dried at the bottom (washing out your bottles as soon as the
beer inside them has been drunk will save you a lot of time
and effort later on). If the bottles are very soiled, soak them in
a light bleach solution for an hour. Then remove the dirt and
debris using a bottle brush, and sanitize and rinse the bottles.

Bottle brushes

ACID-BASED STERILIZERS

Suitable for use on most materials, including stainless steel, acid-based sterilizers are easy to use, work very quickly—often in as little as 30 seconds—and require minimum rinsing. In fact, the most popular brand, a foaming product called Star San, doesn't need to be rinsed off at all. Star San can be less effective if your water is hard and has high alkalinity. If the solution is cloudy after mixing or has a pH higher than 3.5, then you will need to use a different water source. Bottled water may be a suitable alternative in these cases.

CHLORINE-BASED STERILIZERS

Products containing chorine are so effective at killing bacteria that only a tiny amount is needed. A solution of just 0.02 fl oz of pure cholorine diluted in 150 gallons of water (or 1 milliliter diluted in 1,000 liters of water) would be adequate. Note that chlorine-based products are not suitable for soaking stainless-steel vessels as they will cause pitting over time. You should also rinse with hot water after use.

Specialty chlorine-based products, in both liquid and powder form, are also available. These are typically very easy to use—just follow individual product usage guidelines.

Household bleach

The most common source of chlorine is household bleach, which is about 5 percent pure chlorine. Prepare a solution of 0.01fl oz of bleach per pint of water (0.5ml of bleach per liter of water) and leave the vessels and equipment to soak for up to 30 minutes. For stubborn residues, use a stronger solution of up to 0.07fl oz per pint (or 3ml per liter) and let soak overnight. Avoid scented bleaches as they can impart unwanted aromas.

IODINE-BASED STERILIZERS

Idophor is the most common iodine-based product and can be a very effective sterilizer. Like chlorine, iodine products will cause pitting on stainless steel if left in contact for extended periods of time. They also have a faint brown color, which can cause staining to plastic products—although this in itself is not a problem.

A NOTE ON SODIUM METABISULFITE

Although some home brewers use sodium metabisulfite (also known as Campden tablets) to sterilize their brewing equipment, the practice is not recommended. Bacteria growth will not be sufficiently inhibited by the chemical, and your beer may still become contaminated.

Sodium metabisulfite is better suited for wine and cider making, in which levels of acidity are higher and the chemical causes sulfur dioxide to be produced (sulfur dioxide is effective at killing off wild bacteria). Wines and ciders typically have higher levels of alcohol, too, which further helps prevent contamination.

Chlorine-based sterilizer (liquid)

Acid-based sterilizer

Chlorine-based sterilizer (powder)

BREWER'S TIP

Scratches in your equipment provide ideal hiding places for bacteria, so make regular checks and replace equipment as necessary.

BREWING **EQUIPMENT**

The basic equipment you need to make beer at home is affordable and can be used for all three methods of brewing—although malt-extract and full-mash brewing do require more equipment than kit brewing.

BREWING EQUIPMENT—AT A GLANCE

Equipment	Kit brewing	Malt-extract brewing	Full-mash brewing
Fermenter (see opposite)	✓	✓	✓
Hydrometer and trial jar (see opposite)	✓	✓	✓
Siphon (see opposite)	✓	✓	✓
Brewer's spoon (see opposite)	✓	✓	✓
Thermometer (see p48)	✓	✓	✓
Storage container (see p48 and p65)	✓	✓	✓
Can opener and kettle (see p48)	✓	N/A	N/A
Airlock (see p48)	OPTIONAL	OPTIONAL	OPTIONAL
Heater (see p48)	OPTIONAL	OPTIONAL	OPTIONAL
Bottle-filling stick (see p48)	OPTIONAL	OPTIONAL	OPTIONAL
Boiler (see p49)	N/A	✓	✓
Weighing scales (see p49)	N/A	✓	✓
Digital timer (see p49)	N/A	✓	✓
Grain bags (see p49)	N/A	OPTIONAL	OPTIONAL
Chiller (see p49)	N/A	OPTIONAL	OPTIONAL
Mash tun (see p50)	N/A	N/A	✓
Sparge arm (see p50)	N/A	N/A	✓
Hot liquor tank (see p50)	N/A	N/A	✓
Hop back (see p51)	N/A	OPTIONAL	OPTIONAL
Erlenmeyer flask (see p51)	N/A	OPTIONAL	OPTIONAL
Stir plate (see p51)	N/A	OPTIONAL	OPTIONAL
Beer gun (see p51)	N/A	OPTIONAL	OPTIONAL
Digital temperature controller and brew fridge (see p51)	N/A	OPTIONAL	OPTIONAL
Brewing software and applications (see p51)	N/A	N/A	OPTIONAL
Digital pH meter (see p51)	N/A	N/A	OPTIONAL
Refractometer (see p51)	N/A	N/A	OPTIONAL

FERMENTATION VESSELS

All home brewers need a suitable fermentation vessel in which to ferment their wort. There are three main types of fermenters:

■ **Plastic "bucket" fermenter**
This is the most popular type. It is inexpensive, durable, easy to clean, and available in several sizes—from 2 gallons (7.5 liters) to over 50 gallons (190 liters). Some plastic fermenters are supplied with an airlock and tap.

■ **Glass carboy**
Also known as a demijohn, the benefits of this popular type of fermenter are that it won't scratch easily, become stained, or taint the beer with unwanted flavors. It also allows you to see the yeast as it ferments. However, glass carboys can be very heavy when full and are awkward to clean.

■ **Stainless-steel fermenter**
This is very hard wearing, easy to clean, and will protect the beer from sunlight. Many have a conical bottom, which allows the yeast to settle out of the wort. They are, however, the most expensive type.

BREWER'S SPOON

A long spoon is essential for stirring large vessels of wort when combining ingredients and for introducing oxygen prior to pitching the yeast. Stainless-steel spoons are easiest to keep clean and free from bacteria.

HYDROMETER AND TRIAL JAR

A hydrometer is an instrument used for measuring the specific gravity, or density, of a liquid. Comprising a glass stem with a scale, and with a weighted bulb at one end, it is placed in a sample of beer (collected in a trial jar) where it floats at a particular level depending on the gravity of the beer. As alcohol is less dense than

sugar—and therefore less buoyant— a hydrometer will float at a lower level as the fermentation process progresses. By taking a reading before fermentation (original gravity or OG) and one afterward (final gravity or FG), you can both determine when fermentation has finished and calculate the alcohol content of the beer (see p63 for more about taking gravity readings and calculating ABV).

SIPHON

A siphon allows you to transfer beer by removing it from the top of a vessel, rather than draining it from the bottom—leaving any sediment undisturbed at the bottom. A siphon can be as simple as a length of plastic tubing. Some types have a sediment trap at one

end, which prevents residue from being sucked up by mistake, and a tap at the other end to control the flow.

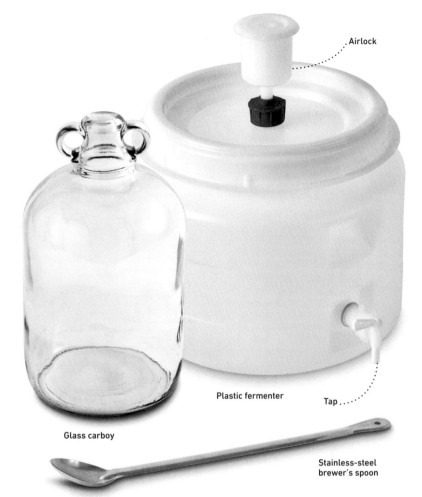

Airlock

Plastic fermenter

Tap

Glass carboy

Stainless-steel brewer's spoon

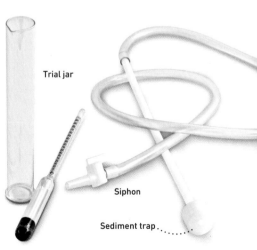

Trial jar

Siphon

Sediment trap

Hydrometer

47

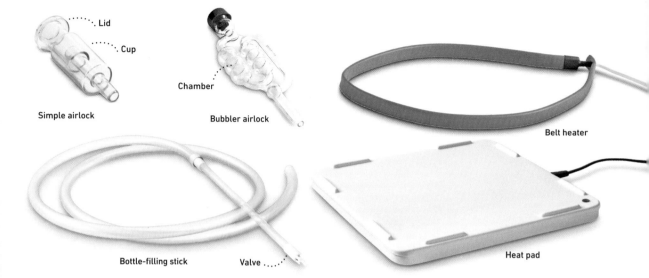

Simple airlock

Lid

Cup

Bubbler airlock

Chamber

Belt heater

Bottle-filling stick

Valve

Heat pad

AIRLOCKS

An airlock is a one-way valve that is fitted to the top of a sealed fermenter using a bung or rubber grommet. It allows carbon dioxide to escape as pressure builds up during fermentation but prevents bacteria in the open air from reaching the wort. There are two main types:

■ **Bubbler airlock**

Also known as a chamber airlock, this consists of a series of water-filled chambers. The water acts as a barrier between the beer and the open air but allows CO_2 to bubble through (meaning you can clearly see when fermentation has begun).

■ **Simple airlock**

Also known as a handy airlock, this type consists of a small plastic cup with a separate lid. The lid dislodges when the pressure in the fermenter builds up, allowing CO_2 to escape, but remains in place over the cup to prevent bacteria from entering. It is easier to clean than a bubbler airlock as the parts can be separated easily and cleaned with a small brush.

BOTTLE-FILLING STICK

Comprising a hollow plastic stick with a valve at the tip, this device releases beer on demand—preventing spillage when bottling.

HEATERS

If the ambient temperature where you intend to ferment your brew is too low, use one of these heaters:

■ **Belt heater**

This wraps around the fermenter. Although the cheapest option, you will not be able to adjust the heat.

■ **Heat pad**

Sit this type of heater on the floor and place the fermenter on top. It heats to a set temperature above the ambient temperature.

■ **Immersion heater**

You will need to submerge this heater into the wort. The most expensive option, it has an adjustable thermostat for accurate temperature control.

THERMOMETERS

All home brewers need a thermometer to monitor the temperature of the wort during fermentation. Malt-extract and full-mash brewers will also need one when preparing hot water for steeping, mashing, and sparging. There are three main types:

■ **Glass spirit thermometer**

This is cheap, accurate, versatile, and the most popular type.

■ **Self-adhesive thermometer**

This liquid-crystal thermometer can be fixed to the outside of the fermenter for easy monitoring.

■ **Digital thermometer**

This is the easiest type of thermometer to use and read but is also the most expensive.

STORAGE CONTAINER

All brewers will need a container (or containers) in which to store their beer while it matures. This could be a pressure barrel, keg, cask, or bottles (see pp64–65 for more about storage).

CAN OPENER AND KETTLE

Kit brewers will need a can opener (most kits are in canned form) and a kitchen kettle or brew pot for adding boiling water to the fermenter when dissolving the malt extract.

Additional equipment for malt-extract and full-mash brewing

BOILERS

For malt-extract and full-mash brewing, you will need a vessel in which to boil large volumes of liquid. Boilers may be made from plastic (cheap and easy to clean), stainless steel (hard wearing and easy to clean), or enamel (hard wearing and won't become stained). You should choose a boiler with enough "head space" at the top to avoid boilovers—to boil a 6-gallon (23-liter) batch, you will need a boiler with a capacity of 8 gallons (30 liters). Heat is provided by a built-in electric element or via a separate gas burner (most kitchen gas stoves are not powerful enough to maintain a vigorous boil).

CHILLER

A chiller enables you to cool large volumes of hot wort quickly and efficiently. A rapid cool reduces the risk of bacterial infection and creates a "cold break," in which proteins in the wort coagulate and sink to the bottom of the boiler where they are less likely to be transferred to the fermenter. There are two main types of chillers:

■ Immersion chiller

This comprises a coil of copper or stainless-steel piping that you submerge in the hot wort. Tubing connected to each end of the coil allows cold water to be passed through for cooling. It can chill 6 gallons (23 liters) of near-boiling wort to fermentation temperature (about 68°F/20°C) in about 30 minutes.

■ Counterflow chiller

This consists of a series of metal plates mounted inside a sealed unit. You pass cold water through

Stainless-steel boiler

Built-in electric element

Plastic boiler

Copper piping

Plastic tubing

Immersion chiller

a channel on one side of the unit and hot wort through a separate channel on the other side of the unit. The metal plates in between act as heat exchangers and cool the wort. Counterflow chillers may require an additional pump, are difficult to clean, and are more expensive than immersion chillers.

WEIGHING SCALES

You will need to weigh out each grain and hop addition for malt-extract and full-mash recipes. Digital scales are sensitive enough

to give precise measurements for very small hop additions.

DIGITAL TIMER

This is used to remind you when to make each hop addition.

GRAIN BAGS

Grain bags are a convenient way of adding and removing speciality grains when steeping.

Additional equipment for full-mash brewing

MASH TUN

A mash tun is the vessel in which you combine and steep grains and hot water during the mash (see p57). A good mash tun should be well insulated and capable of maintaining a constant temperature for the duration of the mash—losing no more than 1.8°F (1°C) over a 90-minute period. Many mash tuns are simply plastic picnic-style coolers fitted with a tap and a grain strainer. These are widely available from home-brew suppliers. Alternatively, you could customize a cooler yourself. Stainless-steel tuns are harder wearing and easier to keep clean than plastic ones.

ROTATING SPARGE ARM

Used for rinsing the grains during the sparge (see p58), a rotating sparge arm works just like a sprinkler. Made of a hollow stainless-steel tube with tiny holes along its length, it rotates freely when you flow sparge water through it, adding a fine spray across the surface of the grain. A support bar allows it to be placed across the top of the mash tun.

HOT LIQUOR TANK (HLT)

This vessel is used to heat and store the brewing liquor, or water, required for the various stages of full-mash

brewing—the mash, sparge, and boil (see pp56–59). Although you can use a boiler (see p49) to heat and store water, too, it is usually quicker and more convenient to use a separate vessel. A hot liquor tank is particularly useful, for example, if you are treating your liquor beforehand (see pp34–35), as it allows you to prepare and store the total volume in advance. For this reason, the HLT will need to be larger than the boiler, although the heating system doesn't have to be as powerful since it will be used only to heat water to mash and sparge temperature and not to a boil.

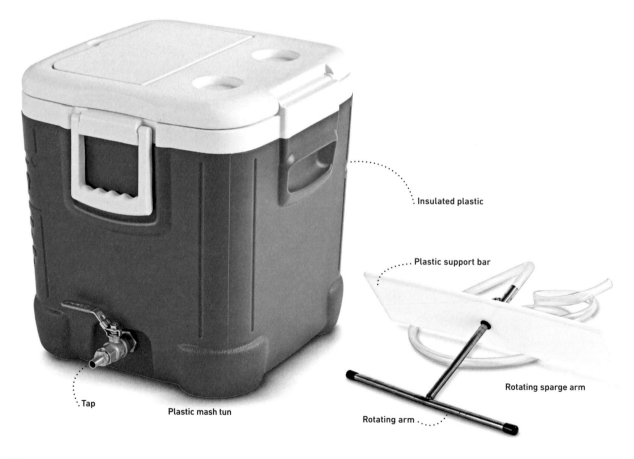

Insulated plastic

Plastic support bar

Rotating sparge arm

Tap

Plastic mash tun

Rotating arm

Advanced equipment

REFRACTOMETER
Accurate and simple to use, this is an optical instrument used to measure the density of a liquid based on its refractive index. You need only add a few drops of liquid to the device's optical prism, and you can use it instead of a hydrometer and trial jar (see p47) to determine the specific gravity of your beer. Most refractometers automatically adjust for temperature, making them ideal for taking gravity readings of hot wort while sparging (see p58). Avoid using refractometers during fermentation, as the alcohol will interfere with the reading.

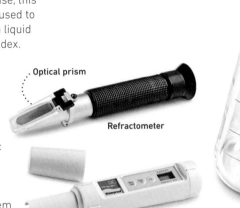

Optical prism

Refractometer

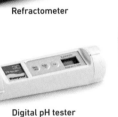

Digital pH tester

Erlenmeyer flask

Hop back

DIGITAL PH TESTER
Advanced full-mash brewers will find it useful to be able to measure the acidity of the mash. Digital pH testers are simple to use and calibrate, give an accurate reading, and are easier to read than paper pH tester strips.

ERLENMEYER FLASK
An Erlenmeyer flask—named after the German chemist Emil Erlenmeyer—is a conical-shaped vessel useful for making yeast starters (see pp60–61). It allows you to combine, heat, and ferment the starter in a single vessel, and the conical shape means you can shake it to introduce oxygen without the contents spilling out. Choose a flask that is at least 0.3 gallons (1 liter) larger than the starter volume.

HOP BACK
A hop back is a type of infuser used for extracting delicate hop oils and aromas that would otherwise be lost during the boil. At the end of the boil, you divert the wort through the unit before running it into a counterflow chiller (see p49), where the wort is cooled and the aromas "locked-in." Used mainly by micro- and commercial brewers, hop backs are extremely effective at delivering a strong hoppy character from a small amount of hops. A version specially developed for home brewing—called the HopRocket—will allow you to achieve professional results.

DIGITAL TEMPERATURE CONTROLLER AND BREW FRIDGE
By controlling the fermentation temperature, you can create a wide range of beer styles and achieve consistent results. Many home brewers store the fermenter in an old fridge that has been fitted with a heater—both are then connected to a temperature controller. The controller can turn on either the fridge or heater as required.

BREWING SOFTWARE AND APPLICATIONS
When creating your own malt-extract or full-mash beer recipes, computer software and applications are ideal for making the necessary bitterness, color, and gravity calculations. Many applications create worksheets that help you plan your brew day, and some even produce shopping lists of ingredients (see p219 for details of online resources).

STIR PLATE
Made of a metal bar, which is placed inside a fermentation vessel where it is moved by magnetic force, this is used to continuously agitate liquid-yeast starters (see pp60–61).

BEER GUN
This device allows you to transfer beer that has been stored and carbonated in a keg to bottles, without the need to add priming sugar (see p64)—thereby minimizing sediment.

USING A **KIT**

Home-brew kits are a great introduction to the brewing process.
They are quick, easy, and require only basic knowledge. With a little
care, a kit will produce great-tasting beer in a matter of weeks.

Most kits make about 6 gallons (23 liters) of beer, although stronger beers
may be brewed in smaller volumes for greater concentration and a higher
starting gravity. Before you begin, check that all the ingredients are present
and within their use-by dates and that you have the right equipment. Read the
instructions and check how much water needs to be added.

THREE MAIN TYPES OF KITS

■ One-can liquid kits consist of a single can (or plastic pack) of hopped malt
extract. These require extra sugar or malt extract to increase the amount of
fermentable sugars to reach the correct starting gravity.
■ Two-can liquid kits (see step-by-step sequence) contain twice the amount
of liquid malt and do not require additional sugar. They produce fuller-bodied,
more professional-tasting beers than other types of kits.
■ Dried-malt kits contain powdered malt extract and may require additional
sugar or malt extract. Always check the instructions first.

EQUIPMENT

Large pan
Can opener
Fermenter
Brewer's spoon or paddle
Hydrometer and trial jar
Thermometer
Airlock (optional)

INGREDIENTS

1 or 2 cans liquid malt extract, or
1 packet dried malt (as supplied)
1 packet brewer's yeast
Additional sugar, malt extract,
hops, or fruit (if required)

PREPARATION 20 MINS

1 Place the cans of malt extract in a pan of hot water. This
will soften the liquid and make it easier to pour. While the
cans are warming, thoroughly sterilize all your equipment
(see pp44–45).

2 Open the cans and empty the contents into the fermenter.
Add a kettleful of boiling water to the fermenter. Put on a
pair of oven gloves and rinse out the cans with a little extra
boiling water.

MAKING THE WORT 10 MINS

3 Add cold water to make up the required volume, pouring it in from a height to create a splash, then stir vigorously. This will oxygenate the wort and encourage the yeast to multiply quickly for healthy fermentation.

4 Take a sample of the wort with a sterilized trial jar (you could use a "beer thief" or turkey baster, if you have one, to extract the wort). Take a reading with a hydrometer (see p63)—this is the original gravity.

PITCHING THE YEAST 5 MINS

5 Measure the temperature of the wort in the fermenter. If it is warmer than 75°F (24°C), close the lid and wait for it to cool before moving to step 6 and pitching (adding) the yeast. If the wort is too hot, you could kill off the yeast cells.

6 Open the packet of yeast and sprinkle it evenly over the surface of the wort. Check the instructions and, if required, add any sachets of hops or fruit. Close the lid of the fermenter, fit an airlock (if using), and let ferment.

See pp62–63 for more about fermentation

53

USING **MALT** EXTRACT

Malt-extract brewing takes a little more time than using a kit (see pp52–53), but the use of fresh hops and specialty grains helps create a fuller-flavored, more aromatic beer.

Many people start their brewing career using the malt-extract method. This involves boiling unhopped malt extract with hops. The key to making great beer is always to use very fresh ingredients.

The malt-extract recipes in this book use dried malt extract, which dissolves readily in cold water; liquid malt extract, if you decide to use it, dissolves better in hot water.

HOW MUCH WORT TO BOIL?

It is best to boil the total volume of wort 7 gallons (27 liters) if you can. However, if you prefer to boil a smaller volume, use 2.6 gallons (10 liters) of water and just 2lb 3oz (1kg) of dried malt extract. This will keep the gravity of the wort low—as it would have been if you had boiled the total volume—and so allow the hops to impart the correct level of bitterness. Ten minutes before the end of the boil, add the balance of malt extract, and top off the fermenter with cold water when ready.

EQUIPMENT

Weighing scales
Boiler or large pan
Thermometer
Grain bag (optional)
Brewer's spoon or paddle
Chiller (optional)
Fermenter
Hydrometer and trial jar
Airlock (optional)

INGREDIENTS

Malt extract (dried or liquid)
Hops
Brewer's yeast

PREPARATION 30 MINS

If adding grains, use a thermometer to take the temperature of the water

1 Planning is key for a successful brew day, so create a worksheet detailing every grain and hop addition. Make sure all your equipment is sterilized (see pp44–45), then weigh out each grain and hop addition.

2 Measure the required volume of water into a boiler or large pan, and turn on the heat. If the recipe calls for steeped grains, heat the water to 160°F (70°C). If not, bring the water to a boil and jump to step 4, opposite.

Using a grain bag makes it easier to remove the grains later on

Watch the pan closely as you boil the malt extract—in case the wort boils over

3 Add the grains to the water (use a grain bag if you have one). Close the boiler or pan lid and let infuse for 30 minutes. Keep the temperature at 149–158°F (65–70°C). Strain the grains (or remove the bag) and bring the water to a boil.

4 Once the water is boiling, remove the pan from the heat and add the malt extract (if using dried, dissolve it in a little cold water first). Stir well to remove any lumps, then bring the wort to a vigorous boil.

BOILING AND COOLING THE WORT 1 HR 30 MINS–2 HR

Allow the wort to cool a little before adding any aroma hops

5 Add the first batch of hops (for bittering) and set a timer to remind you when to make subsequent hop additions (for flavor). Add any aroma hops at the end of the boil, but only once the wort has cooled to 175°F (80°C).

6 Cool the wort quickly using a chiller (see p61), if you have one, or by placing the pan in ice water. Once the wort has cooled to 68–75°F (20–24°C), transfer it to the fermenter, take a hydrometer reading, and pitch the yeast.

See pp60–61 for pitching the yeast

GETTING STARTED USING MALT EXTRACT

FULL-MASH **BREWING**

This advanced method requires the most equipment, skill, and
knowledge but is still achievable for the novice home brewer.
There are three key stages—the mash, the sparge, and the boil.

STAGE 1—THE MASH
The mash (see opposite) involves steeping malt in hot water (liquor) for
1 hour—although there is no harm in leaving it for longer. This dissolves the
starches in the grains and converts them into fermentable sugars.

STAGE 2—THE SPARGE
The sparge (see p58) involves rinsing the steeped grains to extract as many
of the fermentable sugars as possible. The sweet wort obtained during the
sparge is then transferred to the boiler.

STAGE 3—THE BOIL
The boil (see p59) involves bringing the wort to a vigorous boil and adding
hops at various intervals as required by the recipe. The boil should last for
at least an hour, during which time the wort is sterilized and the hops
impart the right amount of bitterness, flavor, and aroma.

EQUIPMENT

Weighing scales
Boiler
Hot liquor tank (optional)
Mash tun
Sparge arm and tubing
Brewer's spoon or paddle
Hydrometer and trial jar
Airlock
Chiller

INGREDIENTS

Grains
Hops
Irish moss (or protofloc)

PREPARATION UP TO 1 HR

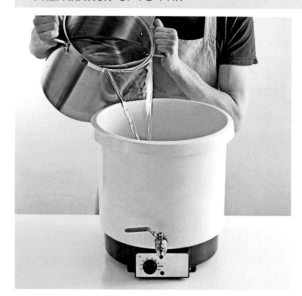

Pale malt

Amber malt

Flaked corn

Hops

Irish moss

1 Add the total liquor to the boiler or HLT and heat to 171°F
(77°C). This may take up to 1 hour, depending on your
boiler. For convenience, and if using an HLT with a timer,
set it to come on before the start of your brew day.

2 Prepare ahead for a stress-free brew day. Weigh out the
ingredients in advance, including any Irish moss (or
protofloc, if using), and label each hop addition and time.
Add some hot liquor to the mash tun to warm it up.

Stage 1—the mash

The ideal temperature for the mash is 149–154°F (65–68°C). The high end of this range produces less fermentable sugars—for sweeter, weaker beers; the low end produces more fermentable sugars—for drier, stronger beers. Use 0.7 gallons (2.5 liters) of hot water per 2¼lb (1kg) of grain. This will allow you to add extra hot or cold water to adjust the temperature as needed.

THREE MAIN TYPES OF MASHES

■ Single-stage infusion mashing (see below) involves holding the temperature constant for the duration of the mash. This is the simplest and most popular method among both commercial and home brewers.

■ Multi-rest mashing involves starting the mash at a low temperature, before increasing and holding the temperature and then increasing and holding it again. This increases the sugar yield from the malt.

■ Decoction mashing involves increasing the temperature in stages by removing a portion of grain, boiling it separately, and then returning it to the main mash. This can be done in one, two, or three stages (single-, double-, or triple-decoction mashing) and produces extra malt characters.

STUCK MASH

Be careful not to overstir the grains as you combine them in the mash tun—this can cause a "stuck" mash. A stuck mash is when the runoff during the sparge is very slow, or when the mash tap becomes completely blocked, making it impossible to transfer the wort to the boiler. If this happens, gently stir the grain to agitate it and then let it settle. Don't worry if the additional time needed to do this means the grains are in the mash tun for more than 1 hour, as it will not affect the character of the final brew.

SINGLE-STAGE INFUSION MASHING APPROX 1 HR

3 Add the hot liquor and the grains to the mash tun—this is known as "doughing-in." Add the required liquor via the tap on the boiler or HLT, then pour in the grains very slowly to avoid creating lumps or dry areas.

4 Break up any lumps by slicing the mash in a gentle side-to-side motion using a spoon. Do not overstir. Close the lid and leave for 1 hour. Meanwhile, check that the liquor left in your boiler or HLT is still at 171°F (77°C).

See pp58–59 for the sparge and boil

Stage 2—the sparge

Once the grains have infused, you will need to rinse the fermentable sugars from the mash and run the wort into the boiler. This is known as sparging. The water for sparging should be 165–171°F (74–77°C)—any higher, and tannins from the grains will be dissolved, creating harsh, astringent flavors; any lower, and the runoff will be less fluid and fewer sugars will be extracted. Prepare at least 5.2 gallons (20 liters) of sparge water.

THREE MAIN SPARGING METHODS

■ Continuous sparging (see below) extracts the most amount of sugar from the grains. It involves adding a spray of water to the surface of the grains while draining an equal volume of wort from the bottom of the tun.

■ Batch sparging involves adding hot water to the mash, stirring, and letting infuse for 20 minutes. A runoff is then taken and returned to the mash to filter any grain debris. When the runoff is clear, the wort is drained into the boiler and the process repeated.

■ With the no-sparge method, the wort is run directly into the boiler. Although this is the easiest method, a lot of sugar will be left behind.

OVERSPARGING

Be careful not to oversparge. If your runnings drop below a specific gravity of 1010 when you take a reading, it means there is a likelihood that tannins are starting to be extracted from the grain. This will affect the quality of the finished beer.

To check the gravity of hot wort, when it is hot, add a drop or two to a refractometer (see p51) if you have one. This will automatically adjust for the high temperature.

CONTINUOUS SPARGING 30–40 MINS

5 Collect a runoff from the mash tap and pour it back over the grain, repeating until the wort runs clear. Set up the sparge arm and connect it to the hot liquor tank (HLT) with tubing. Run a second tube from the mash tap to the boiler.

6 Open the HLT tap to begin sparging. Now open the mash tap to run hot wort into the bottom of the boiler, making sure not to splash the wort. Continue sparging until your boiler contains about 7 gallons (27 liters) of wort.

Stage 3—the boil

With your boiler now containing the correct volume of wort, bring the brew to a rolling boil and add the hops according to the recipe. During the boil, alpha acids, flavors, and aromas are extracted from the hops (see pp26–29 for more about hops). The boil also sanitizes the wort, concentrates it, and helps get rid of unwanted proteins (see right).

COOLING THE WORT

■ At the end of the boil, you will need to cool the wort as quickly as possible to the correct temperature for pitching the yeast. A rapid cool prevents the wort from being contaminated and doesn't hold up your brew day. The most effective way to cool the wort at the end of the boil is to use an immersion chiller (see p49 and step 8, below). This will cool the wort to fermentation temperature (68°F/20°C) in about 20 minutes. Sterilize the chiller by placing it in the boiler for the last 10 minutes of the boil.

■ If you don't have a chiller—and are not using a boiler with an electric element—you can place the boiler in a bath of ice-cold water. This is the easiest method, but it will take at least an hour to cool a full batch of wort.

THE HOT AND COLD BREAK

The high temperature of the rolling boil will create a "hot break," and the rapid reduction in temperature when cooling will create a "cold break." This occurs when proteins in the wort are forced out of suspension in the liquid, coagulate, and then drop to the bottom of the boiler. These breaks prevent proteins from being transferred to the fermenter, which can cause "chill haze" in the finished beer.

BOILING AND COOLING THE WORT 1½–2 HR

Be careful— the output water from the chiller can be very hot

7 Bring the wort to a rolling boil and wait for the hot break before adding the first batch of hops (for bittering). Then follow the boil schedule in the recipe, adding hops (for flavor and aroma) as directed.

8 Lower the chiller into the wort toward the end of the boil. When ready, flow cold water slowly through it. When the wort reaches 68–72°F (20–22°C), transfer it to the fermenter, fully opening the boiler tap to oxygenate the wort.

See pp60–61 for pitching the yeast

PITCHING THE **YEAST**

Regardless of how the wort is produced, all home brewers must pitch, or add, yeast to start fermentation. After a few days, your recipe may require more hops. This is known as dry hopping.

Pitching the correct level, or amount, of yeast is key to healthy fermentation. Underpitching will put strain on the yeast, lengthen the lag time (see p62), and increase the chances of infection. Overpitching can introduce unwanted flavors and decrease head retention. The level of yeast required depends on the volume, gravity, and temperature:

■ One packet of dried yeast is enough to ferment 6 gallons (23 liters).
■ Higher gravity beers (those over 1060) contain more fermentable sugars and require more yeast. Use 2 packets per batch.
■ Use 2 packets per batch when fermenting at lower temperatures.

YEAST STARTERS

A liquid-yeast starter is a solution of liquid yeast, dried malt extract (DME), and water that is allowed to ferment. The aim is to propagate the yeast cells prior to pitching for improved fermentation. See p219 for details of online calculators to help you determine the required starter volume.

DRIED VS. LIQUID YEAST

• Dried yeast keeps well and can be sprinkled directly into the wort. As long as it is within its use-by date and stored in a cool place, it should contain enough live cells to ferment a typical batch of beer.

• In contrast, the number of live cells in liquid yeast decreases over time. Most must be used within 4 months, but the older they are, the less viable the yeast will be. A typical liquid yeast contains enough live cells to ferment just 4.7 gallons (18 liters), so it is best to use a yeast starter (see below).

MAKING A LIQUID-YEAST STARTER 15 MINS, PLUS 2 DAYS' FERMENTATION

1 Find a vessel that holds 1¾ pints (1 liter) more than the starter volume. An Erlenmeyer, or conical, flask is ideal as you can use it to both boil and chill the starter. Dissolve the DME (3½oz/100g for a 1¾-pint/1-liter starter) in water.

2 Top up the flask with water to the required volume and bring to a boil. After 15 minutes, remove from the heat and cool in ice water (if not using a flask, boil the starter in a pan, then add the cooled wort to a sterilized vessel).

DRY HOPPING

Dry hopping involves adding fresh hops to the fermenter a few days after pitching the yeast—once primary fermentation (see p62) is complete. Dry hopping has the benefit of introducing powerful hop aromas from a relatively small amount of hops. This is because the aromas and essential oils are not driven off, either by the heat of the boil or by the carbon dioxide produced during primary fermentation.

■ Dry hop about 4 days after pitching the yeast, when alcohol will be present in the beer—alcohol will kill off any bacteria from the hops—and very little carbon dioxide is being produced.

■ Use a hop bag to avoid particles being transferred to the finished beer. A bag also makes removing the hops far easier.

■ Remove the dry hops after about 1 week. Any longer and they may introduce an unwanted, grassy character to the beer.

■ Use 1–1¾oz (25–50g) for a typical batch, although this will depend on the strength of the particular hop variety—feel free to experiment.

■ Dry hops can be added to beers created using a kit, malt extract, or the full-mash method.

FINING AGENTS

Finings are added during the brewing process to help clarify the beer. They cause particles suspended in the liquid to clump together and sink to the bottom of the fermenter, where they are less likely to be transferred to the finished beer. Finings are added at 2 key stages:

• During the last 10–15 minutes of the boil, when they are known as copper finings (the "copper" being the traditional name for the boiler). Copper finings, such as Irish moss and protofloc, prevent proteins from the malt being transferred to the fermenter and are highly recommended.

• After fermentation is complete, to speed up the final stage of clearing. Commercial brewers add finings to decrease the time taken for the beer to settle after transportation. For home brewers, however, it comes down to personal choice as gravity will clear your beer in time. Isinglass, produced from the swim bladders of fish, is a popular choice but means the beer is no longer vegan.

3 Add the yeast then cover the flask or vessel with foil and shake well. Leave for about 2 days, periodically shaking to introduce plenty of oxygen. Once fermentation is complete, allow the yeast sediment to settle.

4 Pour off and discard all the liquid before pitching the yeast. Once the wort in your fermenter has cooled to 68–75°F (20–24°C), add the yeast sediment, close the fermenter lid, and add an airlock (if using).

THE FERMENTATION **PROCESS**

Once you have produced a wort and pitched the yeast, the next stage of the brewing process is fermentation—when the sweet, nonalcoholic liquid is transformed into beer.

THREE STAGES OF FERMENTATION

■ There are three key phases of fermentation. The first is the lag or adaptive phase, when the yeast cells start to multiply. The wort is easily contaminated at this point, so the shorter the lag, the better—ideally no more than 24 hours. After this time, a cream-colored head, or krausen, should form.

■ The second stage is the primary or attenuative phase—when the yeast ferments the sugars in the wort and produces, among other things, alcohol and carbon dioxide. This usually takes a few days, during which time the gravity will decrease and the krausen will subside. It is normal to notice a dirty residue, floating particles, and even a pungent smell at this point.

■ Finally, there is the secondary or conditioning phase, when the yeast removes any unwanted by-products (natural chemical compounds such as esters and diacetyl). This helps create a clear, clean-tasting beer.

OXYGEN AND TEMPERATURE

During the lag phase, the presence of oxygen is crucial—without it, the yeast cells would be unable to multiply effectively. For the home brewer, lots of splashing and stirring just before pitching the yeast should be enough to introduce the required amount of oxygen. It is important to note, however, that this is the only time during the whole brewing process when oxygen should be introduced.

Keeping the wort at the correct temperature will promote healthy yeast growth and provide a suitable environment for fermentation. Each yeast strain performs best within a particular temperature range, and by working within this range, a brewer can modify the final taste of the beer. Lower temperatures usually result in cleaner-tasting beers, while warmer temperatures tend to produce additional flavor compounds—either outcome may be desirable.

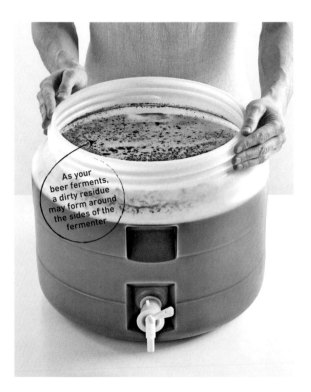

As your beer ferments, a dirty residue may form around the sides of the fermenter

TIPS FOR HEALTHY FERMENTATION

• Before pitching the yeast, make sure plenty of oxygen has been introduced to the wort. You can do this by splashing the cooled wort into the fermenter after the boil and then stirring vigorously.

• To help kick-start fermentation, always start off at a slightly higher temperature than stated in the recipe. You can then decrease the temperature when signs of fermentation are visible.

• Always pitch the correct amount of healthy yeast—too little, and fermentation may stall, and too much may introduced off-flavors (see p60 for pitching levels).

USING A HYDROMETER TO TAKE A GRAVITY READING 5 MINS

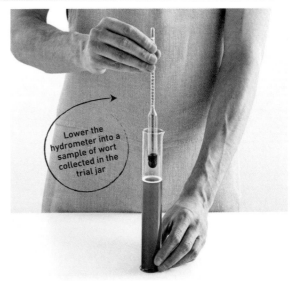

Lower the hydrometer into a sample of wort collected in the trial jar

1 Taking a gravity reading using a hydrometer is the only accurate way of knowing when fermentation is complete (when the reading matches the expected final gravity). To do this, first take a sample of wort using a sterilized trial jar.

2 Holding the hydrometer at the top of the stem, lower it into the sample. When the hydrometer reaches its point of equilibrium, carefully let go, then wait for it to settle. If bubbles are obscuring the scale, gently turn the stem to release them.

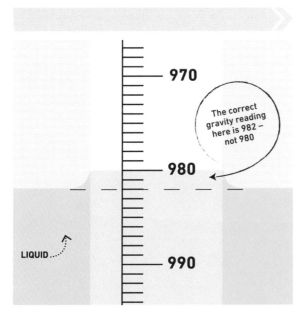

The correct gravity reading here is 982 – not 980

970

980

990

LIQUID

3 Take the reading at eye level, reading the scale at the same plane as the horizontal surface of the liquid—not at the point where the liquid rises up as it touches the stem of the hydrometer.

HOW TO CALCULATE ABV

As well as indicating when fermentation is complete, gravity readings can be used to calculate how much sugar has been converted to alcohol, and so determine the strength of your brew. You will need to take a reading before pitching the yeast (the original gravity or OG) and a second reading before bottling or barreling (the final gravity or FG). Multiplying the difference between these two readings by 105 will give you the percentage of alcohol by weight. To determine the percentage of alcohol by volume (ABV)—the measure used by most commercial brewers—simply multiply the alcohol-by-weight figure by 1.25. So, for example:

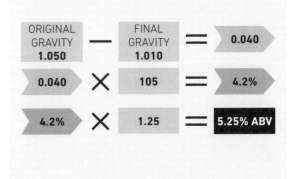

| ORIGINAL GRAVITY 1.050 | − | FINAL GRAVITY 1.010 | = | 0.040 |

| 0.040 | × | 105 | = | 4.2% |

| 4.2% | × | 1.25 | = | 5.25% ABV |

PRIMING, RACKING, AND STORING

Beer is primed with sugar to achieve the right level of carbonation. It is then racked—transferred to barrels, kegs, or bottles—and left to condition, which allows the liquid to clear and the flavors to mature.

Beers such as lager and wheat beer are best served highly carbonated and with a large head. Ales, which appear quite flat, still require the right amount of CO_2 to produce a small head and a slight tingle on the tongue.

To carbonate your beer, you will need to add a small amount of fermentable sugar prior to racking.

CALCULATING PRIMING SUGAR QUANTITIES

The amount of sugar needed depends on the type of sugar being used, the size of the batch of beer, and the desired level of carbonation. The most common sugars are corn (or brewing) sugar, cane sugar, and dried malt extract (DME). The chart below shows the level of carbon dioxide required for each beer style (shown as a ratio of volumes of CO_2 per volume of beer) and the amount of sugar needed to achieve this level of carbonation. It assumes a storing temperature of 68°F (20°C).

PRIMING SOLUTION

The best way to prime your beer is to make a solution by dissolving the sugar or DME in a little boiling water. Allow it to cool, add it to the fermenter, and then stir gently with a sterilized spoon, being careful not to disturb the sediment.

Making a solution will help evenly distribute the sugar. The method is also more accurate than adding sugar directly to each bottle. This is important, since an overprimed bottle is at risk of exploding.

CARBONATION PRIMING CHART

Beer style	CO₂ (Volumes of CO_2 per volume of beer)	Corn sugar (Weight required per 6-gallon/23-liter batch)	Cane sugar (Weight required per 6-gallon/2- liter batch)	DME (Weight required per 6-gallon/23-liter batch)
Light lagers, bock, pale ale, and fruit beers	2.5	5.3oz (150g)	5oz (142g)	8.1oz (230g)
Amber lager; light and amber hybrids	2.4	4.9oz (140g)	4.7oz (133g)	7.6oz (215g)
Dark lager	2.6	5.6oz (159g)	5.3oz (150g)	8.6oz (244g)
IPA, mild; herb and spice beers	2	3.6oz (102g)	3.5oz (100g)	5.6oz (159g)
Sour and lambic ales; wheat and rye beers	3.75	9.3oz (264g)	8.8oz (250g)	14.3oz (405g)
Bitter	1.5	2oz (57g)	2oz (57g)	3.2oz (90g)
Strong ale	1.9	3.3oz (94g)	3oz (85g)	5.1oz (145g)
Brown ale	1.75	2.9oz (82g)	2.7oz (77g)	4.4oz (125g)
Barley wine	1.8	3oz (85g)	2.9oz (82g)	4.6oz (130g)
Stout and porter	2	3.7oz (105g)	3.5oz (100g)	5.6oz (159g)

RACKING YOUR BEER

Transferring your beer from one vessel to another is known as racking. This may be to another fermenter for extended conditioning in a separate, clean vessel, or to bottles or barrels for storage.

If your fermenter has a tap, simply connect a length of tubing, place the open end of the tube into the desired receptacle, and turn on the tap. If it doesn't have a tap, feed the tubing into the top of the fermenter and siphon the beer. As you siphon, be careful not to disturb the yeast sediment at the bottom of the fermenter as you don't want this to be transferred as well (some siphons have a sediment trap to help prevent this—see p47).

Avoid splashing

Racking must be carried out as carefully as possible, with the minimum of splashing. Splashing will introduce oxygen, which can spoil the flavor of the finished beer and introduce unwanted bacteria. To avoid unnecessary splashing when racking, place the open end of the tubing right at the bottom of the receiving container, and then submerge it once enough beer has been transferred.

STORING YOUR BEER

Your beer needs to be left in a suitable container to condition, and until you want to drink it. There are several storage options available; make sure to clean and sterilize your chosen vessel(s) between each batch.

Bottles

For many home brewers, bottles are the best way to store beer. Available in several sizes and in plastic or glass, they can be refrigerated and are easy to transport. Most require you to add a crown or screw cap, although some have a convenient swing-top stopper. Bottles do, however, take a long time to clean, sterilize, and fill, and will result in high carbonation levels (which is great for lagers and wheat beers but not so good for ales). Avoid using clear bottles as sunlight will react with the hops and cause off-flavors.

ADVANTAGES	DISADVANTAGES
• Easy to store in the refrigerator	• Time-consuming to prepare and fill
• Easy to transport and ideal for giving as gifts	• Better suited for beers served with high levels of carbonation
• Beer will keep for many months	

Bottles

Pressure barrels

These are typically large plastic containers designed to withstand pressure up to about 6 psi (41 kPa). If the pressure exceeds this, a valve in the top allows the brew to vent, preventing possible explosions. Most types of pressure barrels hold up to 6.5 gallons (25 liters) of beer. Priming sugar is added to the beer prior to barreling (see opposite), and, as the beer is drunk and the pressure naturally decreases, additional CO_2 can be added via a valve.

Plastic pressure barrel

ADVANTAGES	DISADVANTAGES
• Inexpensive	• May need to be stored in a cool area or fridge to serve beer at the right temperature
• Easy to clean and sterilize	
• Quick and easy to transfer beer from fermenter when racking	• It can be difficult to maintain the correct level of carbonation
• Beer will keep for many months	• There can be some wastage due to dead space below the tap
• Usually fitted with a tap, so no additional equipment required for serving	• Can be difficult to clean

KEG

A keg is a large container for storing and dispensing beer under pressure. It can be connected to a separate CO_2 supply. The most popular type is the stainless steel Cornelius keg (see left), which holds 4.9 gallons (19 liters). It can withstand pressure up to 140 psi (965 kPa) so highly carbonated beers can be served.

ADVANTAGES	DISADVANTAGE
• Durable and easy to clean, sterilize, store, and refrigerate	• Expensive initial setup
• Allow you to control the level of carbonation and are great for serving highly carbonated beers	• More complicated to use
• No priming sugar needs to be added, resulting in less sediment and a shorter conditioning time	• May need to be stored in a cool area or fridge to serve beer at the right temperature
• Beer will keep for many months	
• Limited wastage as beer is drawn from the bottom of the keg	

Cornelius keg

SOURING TECHNIQUES

Fast (wort) souring is a technique used to quickly produce sour-style beers. The most popular method of fast souring among home brewers is kettle souring.

The tart, refreshing character of soured beer is produced by increasing beer's acidity. To do this, the wort is infused with bacteria (usually *Lactobacillus*), which consumes the sugars in the liquid and produces lactic acid. A soured beer will have a pH of around 3.4, compared to around 4.5 for an unsoured beer.

TRADITIONAL SOURING TECHNIQUES

It is likely that, historically, most beers were sour in one way or another. As brewing science and technology improved, this sourness was removed, and sour beers almost ceased to exist. Only a handful of breweries, mostly in and around Belgium, continued to produce sour beer.

Traditionally, bacteria would be introduced to the wort either at the same time as brewer's yeast, or after the primary fermentation was complete. Commonly, beer would be transferred to oak barrels and left for months or often years to mature, since bacteria would have to compete with the yeast for the sugars in the wort. Now that sour beers are being produced once again, it's easy to see why fast-souring techniques are so popular!

HOW TO KETTLE SOUR 24 HRS

1 Perform a standard mash and sparge and collect the wort. Boil the wort for 15 minutes, then allow to cool to 95°F (35°C), or the given temperature for the *Lactobacillus* that you are using.

This step can be skipped if you don't have a pH meter to gauge acidity.

2 Add lactic acid to the wort until it reaches pH4.6. Start by making a small sample pH4.6, then scale up the amount of acid used in order to calculate the total acid needed for the rest of the batch.

THE KETTLE SOUR TECHNIQUE

Of the many fast-souring techniques, kettle souring is the most popular. It requires bacteria to be added to the mash runoff after the sparge has completed and then left until the desired acidity is achieved (usually about 24 hours). The wort is then boiled as usual, a process that kills the bacteria, preventing the beer from becoming any more sour.

In addition to being relatively straightforward to perform, kettle souring has the added advantage of avoiding any interaction between the bacteria and hops. Most *Lactobacillus* strains are not tolerant to the bitterness produced by hops, and so their ability to sour the beer is inhibited when combined. Souring the wort before the boil means that the hops can be added later, without affecting the sourness of the beer.

Avoiding unpleasant flavors

Kettle souring isn't immune from problems, as the warm, sugary wort is a welcome environment for unwanted bacteria. This can cause bad flavors that resemble strong cheese or smelly feet.

To help prevent the wort from harboring these bacteria, sterilize the wort by boiling it for around 15 minutes, lower the pH using lactic acid, and then bubble CO_2 through it to create a barrier against oxygen in the headspace. All of these things mean that the wort becomes a more hostile environment for non-*Lactobacillus* bacteria.

FORMS OF LACTOBACILLUS

There are several forms in which *Lactobacillus* can be bought and added to a wort:

• Lab-grown *Lactobacillus* available at home-brew suppliers
• Homemade wild yeast starter
• Live, nonfat Greek yogurt
• Uncrushed malted barley (although this often introduces unwanted bacteria)

Most strains of *Lactobacillus* work fastest when kept at 86–104°F (30–40°C).

3 Add *Lactobacillus* in the form of powder, yogurt, or home starter. Then cover and insulate your kettle in order to maintain the temperature of the wort while the souring takes place.

4 Bubble a small amount of CO_2 into the wort through a tube or the bottom tap of kettle. Then leave liquid for 24 hours to enable yeast to increase acidity/sourness. When desired sourness is achieved, continue on to the boil.

BEER STYLES
AND RECIPES

RECIPE **CHOOSERS**

Whether you are a dedicated "hophead" or prefer rich, full-bodied beers, use these recipe choosers to find the right beer for you. You'll find all these recipes, and lots more, on pp74–215.

Fruity and zingy beers

Munich Helles (see p77)

Oktoberfest (see p90)

Spring Beer (see p104)

Heather Ale (see p113)

Milkshake IPA (see p131)

Peach IPA (see p133)

Peach and Green Tea Kettle Sour (see p137)

Cherry Lambic (see p138)

Abbey Beer (see p153)

Roggenbier (see p192)

Spiced Honey Beer (see p208)

Spruce beer (see p207)

Raspberry Wheat Beer (see p210)

Strawberry Beer (see p212)

Kiwi Wheat Bear (see p213)

Ginger Beer (see p209)

Spiced Coriander and Lime Beer (see p206)

Nettle Beer (see p215)

Crisp and refreshing beers

Light Lager (see p74)

European Lager (see p76)

Mexican Cerveza (see p80)

Japanese Rice Lager (see p81)

Czech Pilsner (see p82)

Bohemian Pilsner (see p86)

American Pilsner (see p87)

Vienna Lager (see p89)

Helles Bock (see p91)

Black Lager (see p99)

Elderflower Ale (see p105)

East Kent Golding Single-Hop Ale (see p109)

Saaz Single-Hop Ale (see p109)

Kveik Farmhouse Ale (see p117)

English IPA (see p121)

Brett IPA (see p129)

Brut IPA (see p130)

White IPA with Rose and Hibiscus (see p135)

Summer Ale (see p143)

Weissbier (see p187)

Gose (see p189)

American Wheat Beer (see p190)

Raspberry Mosaic Berliner Weisse (see p191)

Witbier (see p195)

Kölsch (see p201)

Raspberry Wheat Beer (see p210)

Raspberry Wheat Beer (see p210)

Witbier (see pp194–195)

Bière de Garde (see p148)

Hoppy beers

Amarillo Single-Hop Ale
(see p108)

Nelson Sauvin Single-Hop Ale (see p108)

Cascade Single-Hop Ale
(see p109)

Double Dry Hopped Pale Ale
(see p120)

New England IPA (see p122)

60-Minute IPA (see p124)

American IPA (see p125)

Imperial IPA (see p126)

Black IPA (see p127)

Rye Beer (see p193)

Rich and full-bodied beers

Traditional Bock
(see p92)

Doppelbock (see p94)

Eisbock (see p95)

Dark American Lager
(see p97)

Munich Dunkel (see p98)

ESB Ale (see p107)

Saison (see p115)

Smoked Beer (see p118)

London Bitter (see p140)

Yorkshire Bitter (see p141)

Cornish Tin Miner's Ale
(see p144)

Scottish 80 Shilling
(see p147)

Irish Red Ale (see p145)

Winter Warmer (see p150)

Christmas Ale (see p151)

Bière de Garde
(see p148)

Belgian Dubbel
(see p155)

Belgian Tripel (see p156)

Belgian Strong Golden Ale (see p157)

Oaked Brown Ale
(see p158)

Northern Brown Ale
(see p160)

Southern Brown Ale
(see p161)

Old Ale (see p163)

Traditional Bock (see p92)

Mild (see p164)

Ruby Mild (see p165)

English Barley Wine
(see p166)

American Barley Wine
(see p168)

Brown Porter (see p169)

Smoked Porter (see p170)

American Stout (see p177)

Milk Stout (see p178)

Russian Imperial Stout
(see p180)

Vanilla Bourbon Stout
(see p181)

Blueberry and Coconut Stout
(see p182)

Coffee, Vanilla, and Maple Imperial Stout (see p183)

LAGERS

The most popular style of beer, lager is consumed in vast quantities around the world. Most nations produce their own variation of the style.

Lager is defined by the type of yeast used during the brewing process. Lager yeast (*Saccharomyces pastorianus*) is bottom fermenting, meaning that it settles to the bottom of the fermenter during fermentation. In contrast, most ale yeasts rise to the surface of the wort (see p108).

LOW TEMPERATURES
Lager yeast performs best at low fermentation temperatures, usually about 54°F (12°C). This is followed by an extended conditioning period, also at low temperatures, which is known as "lagering." The word "lager" comes from the German word *lagern* meaning "to store." The lagering process helps remove many of the flavor compounds produced during fermentation. The result is a clear, crisp-tasting beer with a neutral flavor and a clean finish. Usually, there is little or no hop aroma, although there may be a subtle spiciness. Lager is best served cold and well carbonated.

HOME-BREW LAGER
For the home brewer, lager is one of the most challenging styles to produce well. Not only does it require controlled, cool fermentation conditions, but its subtle, clean character means that any unwanted flavors accidently introduced during the brewing process will be noticeable—however small. That said, it is still possible to brew great lagers by paying proper attention to the fermentation conditions, yeast pitching rates, and cleanliness. The most important factor is temperature control, so investing in a dedicated brew fridge would be wise for the serious lager home brewer.

Light lager

Light lagers have a low alcohol and calorie content, low malt flavor, and a crisp, dry, almost watery finish. They often contain corn or rice.

Appearance Very pale and strawlike in color.

Taste Crisp and dry, often with very little flavor. A dry, cornlike sweetness is sometimes evident.

Aroma A light, spicy hop aroma may be present, although there is often little or no apparent aroma.

Strength 2.8–4.2% ABV

European light lagers are low in alcohol. Since they are brewed wholly with malt—and contain no corn (maize) or rice—they are usually more flavorful than their American counterparts.

American light lagers are very clean and light tasting with few key defining flavors.

See pp74–81

Pilsner

Originating from the Czech city of Plzen˙ (Pilsen), Pilsner is hoppier and has more complex malt flavors than other light lagers.

Appearance Light straw to deep gold in color, with a lasting, creamy, white head.

Taste Has complex malty flavors and a soft bitterness, often with a slightly sweet finish.

Aroma Spicy, floral aromas mixed with a grainy, malt character.

Strength 4.2–6% ABV

Czech Pilsners are lightly flavored and highly carbonated.

German Pilsners have a fairly deep color with a complex malt flavor and bitterness.

American Pilsners are highly hopped but also have a grainy character from the use of corn.

See pp82–87

Amber lager

Toasted malt flavors and aromas dominate this German style, which is traditionally brewed in spring and aged over the summer in caves.

Appearance Dark gold to deep orange in color, crystal clear, and with a lingering, off-white head.

Taste Deep, complex malt flavors are balanced by plenty of hop bitterness.

Aroma A lightly toasted, malty aroma, with little or no hop presence.

Strength 4.5–5.7% ABV

European versions are quite sweet, with complex malt flavors.

American versions are stronger, drier, and have a more assertive hop character.

See pp88–90

Bock and dark lager

Bock is typically dark, strong, and sweet. Other dark lagers range from deep amber to pitch black.

Appearance Deep and intense with a creamy, off-white head.

Taste Bocks are smooth, rich, and caramel-like, with a low hop presence. Other dark lagers may have delicate, burnt flavor notes and a clean, dry, refreshing aftertaste.

Aroma Bocks have a strong toasted malt aroma with little or no hop aroma. Other dark lagers may have hints of chocolate, caramel, or nuts.

Strength 4.2–14% ABV, depending on the style.

There are several bock styles, all from Germany. Traditional bock is sweet, strong, and mildly fruity. Doppelbock is dark, strong, and bitter. Helles bock is paler, less malty, and hoppier.

See pp91–99

Pale straw in color, crisp and refreshing on the palate, this clean-tasting lager is perfect when served chilled. The reduced alcohol content makes this a lower-calorie brew.

LIGHT LAGER

ORIGINAL GRAVITY 1038 EXPECTED FINAL GRAVITY 1011 TOTAL LIQUOR 8.1 GALLONS (30.7 LITERS)

MAKES 6 GALLONS (23 LITERS)	READY TO DRINK 5 WEEKS	ESTIMATED ABV 3.4%	BITTERNESS RATING 9.4 IBU	COLOR RATING 5.5 EBC

FOR THE MASH

LIQUOR 2.5 gallons (9.3 liters) **MASH TIME** 1 hr **TEMPERATURE** 149°F (65°C)

Grain bill	Quantity
US domestic 2-row malt	6lb 3oz (2.81kg)
Flaked corn (maize)	2lb 1oz (939g)

FOR THE BOIL

LIQUOR 7 gallons (27 liters) **BOIL TIME** 1 hr 15 mins

Hops	Quantity	IBU	When to add
Hallertauer Hersbrucker 3.5%	⅔oz (20g)	8.5	At start of boil
Hallertauer Hersbrucker 3.5%	⅓oz (10g)	0.8	For last 5 mins of boil

Other			
Irish moss	1 tsp		For last 15 mins of boil

TO FERMENT

FERMENTATION 54°F (12°C) **CONDITIONING** 4 weeks at 37°F (3°C)

Yeast
Saflager S-189 Dry Lager

BREWER'S TIP

When brewing lagers, it is best to use a large proportion of reverse osmosis (RO) water to help maintain the correct pH levels and avoid "off" flavors.

This golden European-style lager is smooth, full-bodied,
and highly drinkable, with a delicious malty flavor
and a crisp, clean finish.

EUROPEAN LAGER

ORIGINAL GRAVITY 1045 **EXPECTED FINAL GRAVITY** 1015 **TOTAL LIQUOR** 8.8 GALLONS (34 LITERS)

MAKES	READY TO DRINK	ESTIMATED ABV	BITTERNESS RATING	COLOR RATING
6 GALLONS (23 LITERS)	5 WEEKS	4.6%	25.7 IBU	5.6 EBC

FOR THE MASH

LIQUOR 3.6 gallons (14 liters) **MASH TIME** 1 hr **TEMPERATURE** 149°F (65°C)

Grain bill	Quantity
Pilsner malt	8lb 11oz (3.95kg)
Flaked barley	14oz (400g)
Carapils malt	4¾oz (135g)

FOR THE BOIL

LIQUOR 7 gallons (27 liters) **BOIL TIME** 1 hr 15 mins

Hops	Quantity	IBU	When to add
Northern Brewer 8.0%	1oz (26g)	23.8	At start of boil
Hallertauer Hersbrucker 3.5%	½oz (12g)	1.7	For last 10 mins of boil
Hallertauer Hersbrucker 3.5%	½oz (15g)	0.1	For last 1 min of boil

Other			
Irish moss	1 tsp		For last 15 mins of boil

TO FERMENT

FERMENTATION 54°F (12°C) **CONDITIONING** 4 weeks at 37°F (3°C)

Yeast
White Labs WLP830 German Lager

Here, a slightly grainy, malty flavor—from the blend of lightly toasted malts—is balanced by the subtle bitterness and aroma of the spicy Mittelfrüh hops.

MUNICH HELLES

ORIGINAL GRAVITY 1049 **EXPECTED FINAL GRAVITY** 1012 **TOTAL LIQUOR** 8.3 GALLONS (32 LITERS)

MAKES	READY TO DRINK	ESTIMATED ABV	BITTERNESS RATING	COLOR RATING
6 GALLONS (23 LITERS)	5 WEEKS	4.99%	17.1 IBU	6.3 EBC

FOR THE MASH

LIQUOR 3.1 gallons (12 liters)   **MASH TIME** 1 hr   **TEMPERATURE** 149°F (65°C)

Grain bill	Quantity
Pilsner malt	9lb 10oz (4.38kg)
Carapils malt	7oz (200g)
Vienna malt	6oz (175g)

FOR THE BOIL

LIQUOR 7 gallons (27 liters)   **BOIL TIME** 1 hr 15 mins

Hops	Quantity	IBU	When to add
Hallertauer Mittelfrüh 5%	1oz (27g)	14.9	At start of boil
Hallertauer Mittelfrüh 5%	⅔oz (20g)	2.2	For last 5 mins of boil

Other			
Irish moss	1 tsp		For last 15 mins of boil

TO FERMENT

FERMENTATION 54°F (12°C)   **CONDITIONING** 4 weeks at 37°F (3°C)

Yeast
White Labs WLP850 Copenhagen Lager

This is a golden, slightly malty flavored beer with a mild, spicy hop aroma. It finishes with a subtle sweetness and roundness in the mouth.

DORTMUNDER EXPORT

ORIGINAL GRAVITY 1054   **EXPECTED FINAL GRAVITY** 1015   **TOTAL LIQUOR** 8.3 GALLONS (32.2 LITERS)

MAKES	READY TO	ESTIMATED	BITTERNESS	COLOR
6 GALLONS	DRINK	ABV	RATING	RATING
(23 LITERS)	5 WEEKS	5.1%	27.2 IBU	6 EBC

FOR THE MASH

LIQUOR 3.4 gallons (13.1 liters)   **MASH TIME** 1 hr   **TEMPERATURE** 149°F (65°C)

Grain bill	Quantity
Pilsner malt	11lb (5kg)
Munich malt	9oz (250g)

FOR THE BOIL

LIQUOR 7 gallons (27 liters)   **BOIL TIME** 1 hr 15 mins

Hops	Quantity	IBU	When to add
Tettnang 4.5%	1⅓oz (40g)	19.2	At start of boil
Hallertauer Hersbrucker 3.5%	1oz (26g)	3.5	For last 10 mins of boil
Tettnang 4.5%	1oz (26g)	4.5	For last 10 mins of boil
Hallertauer Hersbrucker 3.5%	⅓oz (13g)	0.0	At end of boil

Other			
Irish moss	1 tsp		For last 15 mins of boil

TO FERMENT

FERMENTATION 54°F (12°C)   **CONDITIONING** 4 weeks at 37°F (3°C)

Yeast
Wyeast 2124 Bohemian Lager

Light, crisp, and refreshing, this Mexican-style beer is
sure to hit the spot on a hot summer's day. Serve with
a wedge of lime for an authentic flavor.

MEXICAN CERVEZA

ORIGINAL GRAVITY 1046 **EXPECTED FINAL GRAVITY** 1012 **TOTAL LIQUOR** 8.2 GALLONS (31.5 LITERS)

MAKES	READY TO DRINK	ESTIMATED ABV	BITTERNESS RATING	COLOR RATING
6 GALLONS (23 LITERS)	5 WEEKS	4.6%	23.5 IBU	5.1 EBC

FOR THE MASH

LIQUOR 3 gallons (11.5 liters)   **MASH TIME** 1 hr   **TEMPERATURE** 149°F (65°C)

Grain bill	Quantity
Pilsner malt	8lb 8oz (3.86kg)
Carapils malt	9½oz (270g)
Flaked corn (maize)	1lb (450g)

FOR THE BOIL

LIQUOR 7 gallons (27 liters)   **BOIL TIME** 1hr 15 mins

Hops	Quantity	IBU	When to add
Northern Brewer 8.0%	½oz (14g)	12.5	At start of boil
Crystal 3.5%	⅔oz (18g)	7.1	For last 1 hr of boil
Crystal 3.5%	1oz (28g)	3.9	For last 10 mins of boil

Other			
Irish moss	1 tsp		For last 15 mins of boil

TO FERMENT

FERMENTATION 54°F (12°C)   **CONDITIONING** 4 weeks at 37°F (3°C)

Yeast
White Labs WLP940 Mexican Lager

MALT EXTRACT VERSION

Steep 10½oz (300g) **Carapils malt** in 7 gallons (27 liters)
water at 149°F (65°C) for 30 mins. Remove the malt, then
add 6lb 1oz (2.75kg) **dried light malt extract**, bring to a
boil, and add the hops as specified in the main recipe.

This is an extremely crisp, dry, and well-balanced lager—
thanks to the Sorachi Ace and Saaz hops. As the
name suggests, flaked rice is added to the grain bill.

JAPANESE RICE LAGER

ORIGINAL GRAVITY 1052 **EXPECTED FINAL GRAVITY** 1013 **TOTAL LIQUOR** 8.6 GALLONS (33 LITERS)

MAKES 6 GALLONS (23 LITERS)	READY TO DRINK 5 WEEKS	ESTIMATED ABV 5.3%	BITTERNESS RATING 25 IBU	COLOR RATING 7.3 EBC

FOR THE MASH

LIQUOR 3.4 gallons (13 liters) **MASH TIME** 1 hr **TEMPERATURE** 149°F (65°C)

Grain bill	Quantity
Pilsner malt	10lb 6oz (4.7kg)
Flaked rice	1lb 2oz (500g)

FOR THE BOIL

LIQUOR 7 gallons (27 liters) **BOIL TIME** 1 hr 15 mins

Hops	Quantity	IBU	When to add
Sorachi Ace 14.9%	½oz (13g)	21.0	At start of boil
Sorachi Ace 14.9%	¼oz (5g)	4.0	For last 15 mins of boil
Saaz 4.2%	¼oz (5g)	0.0	At end of boil

Other			
Irish moss	1 tsp		For last 15 mins of boil

TO FERMENT

FERMENTATION 54°F (12°C) **CONDITIONING** 4 weeks at 37°F (3°C)

Yeast
Wyeast 2278 Czech Pils

This refreshing, very pale Pilsner has a distinctive
flavor and aroma—both spicy and floral—which
is imparted by the Czech Saaz hops.

CZECH PILSNER

ORIGINAL GRAVITY 1048 EXPECTED FINAL GRAVITY 1014 TOTAL LIQUOR 8.2 GALLONS (31.6 LITERS)

MAKES	READY TO DRINK	ESTIMATED ABV	BITTERNESS RATING	COLOR RATING
6 GALLONS (23 LITERS)	5 WEEKS	4.4%	25 IBU	5 EBC

FOR THE MASH

LIQUOR 3 gallons (11.6 liters)   **MASH TIME** 1 hr   **TEMPERATURE** 150°F (65°C)

Grain bill	Quantity
Pilsner malt	10lb 4oz (4.66kg)

FOR THE BOIL

LIQUOR 7 gallons (27 liters)   **BOIL TIME** 1 hr 15 mins

Hops	Quantity	IBU	When to add
Czech Saaz 4.2%	1½oz (46g)	21.9	At start of boil
Czech Saaz 4.2%	⅔oz (19g)	3.1	For last 10 mins of boil
Czech Saaz 4.2%	⅔oz (19g)	0.0	At end of boil

Other			
Irish moss	1 tsp		For last 15 mins of boil

TO FERMENT

FERMENTATION 54°F (12°C)   **CONDITIONING** 4 weeks at 37°F (3°C)

Yeast
Wyeast 2278 Czech Pils

MALT EXTRACT VERSION
Add 6lb 10oz (3kg) **dried extra-light malt extract** to
7 gallons (27 liters) water, bring to a boil, and add
the hops as specified in the main recipe.

The strong alcohol flavors in this Pilsner are perfectly balanced by the bitterness of the hops and by the biscuit and Carapils malts.

IMPERIAL PILSNER

ORIGINAL GRAVITY 1079 **EXPECTED FINAL GRAVITY** 1022 **TOTAL LIQUOR** 9.9 GALLONS (38 LITERS)

MAKES 6 GALLONS (23 LITERS)	READY TO DRINK 7 WEEKS	ESTIMATED ABV 7.7%	BITTERNESS RATING 60 IBU	COLOR RATING 10.2 EBC

FOR THE MASH

LIQUOR 4.9 gallons (19 liters)   **MASH TIME** 1 hr   **TEMPERATURE** 149°F (65°C)

Grain bill	Quantity
Pilsner malt	16lb (7.25kg)
Carapils malt	10oz (290g)
Biscuit malt	7oz (200g)

FOR THE BOIL

LIQUOR 7 gallons (27 liters)   **BOIL TIME** 1 hr 15 mins

Hops	Quantity	IBU	When to add
Hallertauer Mittelfrüh 5%	4oz (110g)	25.4	At start of boil
Hallertauer Mittelfrüh 5%	2½oz (73g)	5.9	For last 10 mins of boil
Hallertauer Mittelfrüh 5%	4oz (110g)	0.0	At end of boil

Other			
Irish moss	1 tsp		For last 15 mins of boil

TO FERMENT

FERMENTATION 54°F (12°C)   **CONDITIONING** 6 weeks at 37°F (3°C)

Yeast
Wyeast 2124 Bohemian Lager

MALT EXTRACT VERSION

Steep 10oz (290g) **Carapils malt** and 7oz (200g) **biscuit malt** in 7 gallons (27 liters) water at 149°F (65°C) for 30 mins. Remove the malt, then add 10lb 2oz (4.6kg) **dried extra-light malt extract**, bring to a boil, and add the hops as specified in the main recipe.

BREWER'S TIP

Increase the amount of biscuit malt in the boil—up to 1lb 2oz (500g)—for a more toasted flavor and aroma.

A clean, crisp beer with a fairly bitter hoppiness. These flavor characteristics were traditionally accentuated by the high sulfate content in the German water profile.

GERMAN PILSNER

ORIGINAL GRAVITY 1046 **EXPECTED FINAL GRAVITY** 1012 **TOTAL LIQUOR** 8.2 GALLONS (31.5 LITERS)

MAKES	READY TO DRINK	ESTIMATED ABV	BITTERNESS RATING	COLOR RATING
6 GALLONS (23 LITERS)	5 WEEKS	4.5%	30.2 IBU	5 EBC

FOR THE MASH

LIQUOR 2.9 gallons (11.3 liters)   **MASH TIME** 1 hr   **TEMPERATURE** 149°F (65°C)

Grain bill	Quantity
Pilsner malt	10lb (4.55kg)

FOR THE BOIL

LIQUOR 7 gallons (27 liters)   **BOIL TIME** 1 hr 15 mins

Hops	Quantity	IBU	When to add
Spalt Select 4.5%	1¾oz (50g)	25.7	At start of boil
Spalt Select 4.5%	1oz (25g)	4.5	For last 10 mins of boil
Spalt Select 4.5%	⅔oz (17g)	0.0	At end of boil

Other			
Irish moss	1 tsp		For last 15 mins of boil

TO FERMENT

FERMENTATION 54°F (12°C)   **CONDITIONING** 4 weeks at 37°F (3°C)

Yeast
Wyeast 2007 Pilsen Lager

MALT EXTRACT VERSION
Add 6lb 6oz (2.9kg) **dried extra-light malt extract** to
7 gallons (27 liters) water, bring to a boil, and add
the hops as specified in the main recipe.

With a rich, malty flavor and a lovely spicy, floral aroma from the Saaz hops, this easy-drinking beer is devilishly addictive.

BOHEMIAN PILSNER

ORIGINAL GRAVITY 1051 **EXPECTED FINAL GRAVITY** 1014 **TOTAL LIQUOR** 8.3 GALLONS (32 LITERS)

MAKES	READY TO DRINK	ESTIMATED ABV	BITTERNESS RATING	COLOR RATING
6 GALLONS (23 LITERS)	4–5 WEEKS	4.9%	35.4 IBU	6.9 EBC

FOR THE MASH

LIQUOR 3.3 gallons (12.5 liters) **MASH TIME** 1 hr **TEMPERATURE** 149°F (65°C)

Grain bill	Quantity
Bohemian Pilsner malt	11lb (5kg)

FOR THE BOIL

LIQUOR 7 gallons (27 liters) **BOIL TIME** 1 hr 15 mins

Hops	Quantity	IBU	When to add
Saaz 4.2%	2¾oz (77g)	35.4	At start of boil
Saaz 4.2%	1¼oz (38g)	0.0	At end of boil

Other			
Irish moss	1 tsp		For last 15 mins of boil

TO FERMENT

FERMENTATION 54°F (12°C) **CONDITIONING** 4 weeks at 37°F (3°C)

Yeast
Wyeast 2124 Bohemian Lager

The cornlike maltiness of this golden beer is complemented by a hoppy aroma—a result of the late addition of American hops during the boil.

AMERICAN PILSNER

ORIGINAL GRAVITY 1048 **EXPECTED FINAL GRAVITY** 1012 **TOTAL LIQUOR** 8.3 GALLONS (32 LITERS)

MAKES	READY TO DRINK	ESTIMATED ABV	BITTERNESS RATING	COLOR RATING
6 GALLONS (23 LITERS)	5 WEEKS	4.8%	30.6 IBU	6.4 EBC

FOR THE MASH

LIQUOR 3.1 gallons (12 liters)   **MASH TIME** 1 hr   **TEMPERATURE** 149°F (65°C)

Grain bill	Quantity
US domestic 2-row malt	7lb 11oz (3.5kg)
Flaked corn (maize)	2lb 14oz (1.3kg)

FOR THE BOIL

LIQUOR 7 gallons (27 liters)   **BOIL TIME** 1 hr 15 mins

Hops	Quantity	IBU	When to add
Cluster 7.5%	⅔oz (20g)	16.9	At start of boil
Liberty 4.5%	½oz (15g)	2.7	For last 10 mins of boil
Crystal 3.5%	½oz (15g)	2.1	For last 10 mins of boil
Liberty 4.5%	⅓oz (10g)	1.0	For last 5 mins of boil
Crystal 3.5%	⅓oz (10g)	0.8	For last 5 mins of boil
Liberty 4.5%	1oz (32g)	0.0	At end of boil
Crystal 3.5%	1oz (32g)	0.0	At end of boil

Other			
Irish moss	1 tsp		For last 15 mins of boil

TO FERMENT

FERMENTATION 54°F (12°C)   **CONDITIONING** 4 weeks at 37°F (3°C)

Yeast
Wyeast 2124 Bohemian Lager

This beer has a lightly toasted maltiness and a clean, lager character. The Vienna malt, which is heated to a high temperature during malting, imparts a distinctive flavor.

VIENNA LAGER

ORIGINAL GRAVITY 1050 **EXPECTED FINAL GRAVITY** 1011 **TOTAL LIQUOR** 8.3 GALLONS (32 LITERS)

MAKES	READY TO DRINK	ESTIMATED ABV	BITTERNESS RATING	COLOR RATING
6 GALLONS (23 LITERS)	5 WEEKS	5.1%	26.5 IBU	19.7 EBC

FOR THE MASH

LIQUOR 3.1 gallons (12 liters)   **MASH TIME** 1 hr   **TEMPERATURE** 149°F (65°C)

Grain bill	Quantity
Vienna malt	9lb 3oz (4.16kg)
Munich malt	1lb 7oz (670g)
Melanoidin malt	4½oz (125g)
Chocolate malt	1¾oz (50g)

FOR THE BOIL

LIQUOR 7 gallons (27 liters)   **BOIL TIME** 1 hr 15 mins

Hops	Quantity	IBU	When to add
Northern Brewer 8.0%	1oz (30g)	20.1	At start of boil
Hallertauer Hersbrucker 3.5%	½oz (15g)	0.0	At end of boil
Tettnang 4.5%	½oz (15g)	0.0	At end of boil

Other			
Irish moss	1 tsp		For last 15 mins of boil

TO FERMENT

FERMENTATION 54°F (12°C)   **CONDITIONING** 4 weeks at 37°F (3°C)

Yeast
White Labs WLP830 German Lager

BREWER'S TIP

For a slightly citrus finish, try using the same quantity of Liberty hops at the end of the boil instead of the Tettnang.

This German beer is traditionally brewed in spring, lagered in cold cellars or caves over the summer, and then served at the Oktoberfest celebrations in the fall.

OKTOBERFEST

ORIGINAL GRAVITY 1057 **EXPECTED FINAL GRAVITY** 1017 **TOTAL LIQUOR** 8.3 GALLONS (32 LITERS)

MAKES 6 GALLONS (23 LITERS)	READY TO DRINK 5 WEEKS	ESTIMATED ABV 5.3%	BITTERNESS RATING 25.2 IBU	COLOR RATING 13.6 EBC

FOR THE MASH

LIQUOR 3.1 gallons (12 liters)   **MASH TIME** 1 hr   **TEMPERATURE** 149°F (65°C)

Grain bill	Quantity
Vienna malt	8lb 13oz (4kg)
Munich malt	1lb 12oz (800g)
Carapils	1lb 10oz (750g)
Medium crystal malt	3½oz (100g)

FOR THE BOIL

LIQUOR 7 gallons (27 liters)   **BOIL TIME** 1 hr 15 mins

Hops	Quantity	IBU	When to add
Perle 8.0%	1oz (27g)	23.1	At start of boil
Hallertauer Mittelfrüh 5%	¼oz (5g)	2.1	For last 30 mins of boil

Other			
Irish moss	1 tsp		For last 15 mins of boil

TO FERMENT

FERMENTATION 54°F (12°C)   **CONDITIONING** 4 weeks at 37°F (3°C)

Yeast
White Labs WLP820 Oktoberfest

BREWER'S TIP

This beer will benefit from extended aging at cellar temperatures for as many weeks as you can handle before giving in to temptation!

A recent addition to the Bock family of beers, this brew uses the Hella Bock yeast, which delivers a clean finish and leaves a taste of both malt and hops in the mouth.

HELLES BOCK

ORIGINAL GRAVITY 1072 **EXPECTED FINAL GRAVITY** 1019 **TOTAL LIQUOR** 9.1 GALLONS (35 LITERS)

MAKES	READY TO DRINK	ESTIMATED ABV	BITTERNESS RATING	COLOR RATING
6 GALLONS (23 LITERS)	7 WEEKS	7.1%	32 IBU	17.5 EBC

FOR THE MASH

LIQUOR 4.7 gallons (18 liters)　　**MASH TIME** 1 hr　　**TEMPERATURE** 149°F (65°C)

Grain bill	Quantity
Pilsner malt	8lb 4oz (3.75kg)
Munich malt	5lb 7oz (2.47kg)
Belgian aromatic malt	1lb 5oz (600g)
Melanoidin malt	9oz (250g)

FOR THE BOIL

LIQUOR 7 gallons (27 liters)　　**BOIL TIME** 1 hr 15 mins

Hops	Quantity	IBU	When to add
Northern Brewer 8.0%	1⅓oz (40g)	30.2	At start of boil
Spalt Select 4.5%	⅓oz (10g)	2.0	For last 15 mins of boil
Spalt Select 4.5%	¼oz (8g)	0.0	At end of boil

Other			
Irish moss	1 tsp		For last 15 mins of boil

TO FERMENT

FERMENTATION 54°F (12°C)　　**CONDITIONING** 6 weeks at 37°F (3°C)

Yeast
Wyeast 2487 Hella Bock

BREWER'S TIP

If the Hella Bock yeast is not available, try using Wyeast 2124 Bohemian Lager instead.

First brewed in Einbeck, Germany, in the 1300s,
and later adapted by brewers in Munich, Bock is a dark,
strong, malty lager with a very low hop flavor and aroma.

TRADITIONAL BOCK

ORIGINAL GRAVITY 1064 EXPECTED FINAL GRAVITY 1015 TOTAL LIQUOR 9.1 GALLONS (35 LITERS)

MAKES	READY TO DRINK	ESTIMATED ABV	BITTERNESS RATING	COLOR RATING
6 GALLONS (23 LITERS)	5 WEEKS	6.5%	22 IBU	29.1 EBC

FOR THE MASH

LIQUOR 4.9 gallons (19 liters) **MASH TIME** 1 hr **TEMPERATURE** 149°F (65°C)

Grain bill	Quantity
Pale malt	6lb 1oz (2.75kg)
Munich malt	6lb 1oz (2.75kg)
Carapils malt	1lb 3oz (550g)
Special B malt	12oz (350g)

FOR THE BOIL

LIQUOR 7 gallons (27 liters) **BOIL TIME** 1 hr 15 mins

Hops	Quantity	IBU	When to add
Northern Brewer 8.0%	¾oz (24g)	18.9	At start of boil
Tettnang 4.5%	⅓oz (10g)	3.2	For last 30 mins of boil

Other			
Irish moss	1 tsp		For last 15 mins of boil

TO FERMENT

FERMENTATION 54°F (12°C) **CONDITIONING** 4 weeks at 37°F (3°C)

Yeast
White Labs WLP820 Oktoberfest

Stronger and maltier than Traditional Bock (see p100), this beer was first brewed by monks more than 200 years ago and served as "liquid bread" during times of fasting.

DOPPELBOCK

ORIGINAL GRAVITY 1075 **EXPECTED FINAL GRAVITY** 1021 **TOTAL LIQUOR** 9.1 GALLONS (35 LITERS)

MAKES	READY TO DRINK	ESTIMATED ABV	BITTERNESS RATING	COLOR RATING
6 GALLONS (23 LITERS)	7 WEEKS	7.3%	20.7 IBU	31.8 EBC

FOR THE MASH

LIQUOR 4.9 gallons (18.9 liters) **MASH TIME** 1 hr **TEMPERATURE** 149°F (65°C)

Grain bill	Quantity
Pilsner malt	6lb 3oz (2.8kg)
Munich malt	9lb 4oz (4.20kg)
Caramunich II	10oz (286g)
Carafa special II malt	4oz (114g)

FOR THE BOIL

LIQUOR 7 gallons (27 liters) **BOIL TIME** 1 hr 10 mins

Hops	Quantity	IBU	When to add
Perle 8.0%	⅔oz (20g)	14.4	At start of boil
Tettnang 4.5%	⅔oz (20g)	6.0	For last 30 mins of boil

Other			
Irish moss	1 tsp		For last 15 mins of boil

TO FERMENT

FERMENTATION 54°F (12°C) **CONDITIONING** 6 weeks at 37°F (3°C)

Yeast
Wyeast 2124 Bohemian Lager

Eisbock is a rich, intense brew with a malty flavor and a deep color. It is high in alcohol and has a slight, lingering chocolate flavor on the finish—a beer to be savored.

EISBOCK

ORIGINAL GRAVITY 1113 **EXPECTED FINAL GRAVITY** 1026 **TOTAL LIQUOR** 10.4 GALLONS (40 LITERS)

MAKES	READY TO DRINK	ESTIMATED ABV	BITTERNESS RATING	COLOR RATING
6 GALLONS (23 LITERS)	7 WEEKS	11.8%	30.4 IBU	40 EBC

FOR THE MASH

LIQUOR 7 gallons (27 liters) **MASH TIME** 1 hr **TEMPERATURE** 149°F (65°C)

Grain bill	Quantity
Pale malt	10lb 7oz (4.75kg)
Munich malt	12½lb (5.70kg)
Flaked barley	13½oz (380g)
Chocolate malt	3½oz (100g)
Carafa special I malt	3⅓oz (95g)

FOR THE BOIL

LIQUOR 7 gallons (27 liters) **BOIL TIME** 1 hr 15 mins

Hops	Quantity	IBU	When to add
Northern Brewer 8.0%	1oz (32g)	17.4	At start of boil
Perle 8.0%	1oz (32g)	13.0	For last 30 mins of boil

Other			
Irish moss	1 tsp		For last 15 mins of boil

TO FERMENT

FERMENTATION 54°F (12°C) **CONDITIONING** 6 weeks at 37°F (3°C)

Yeast
Wyeast 2308 Munich Lager

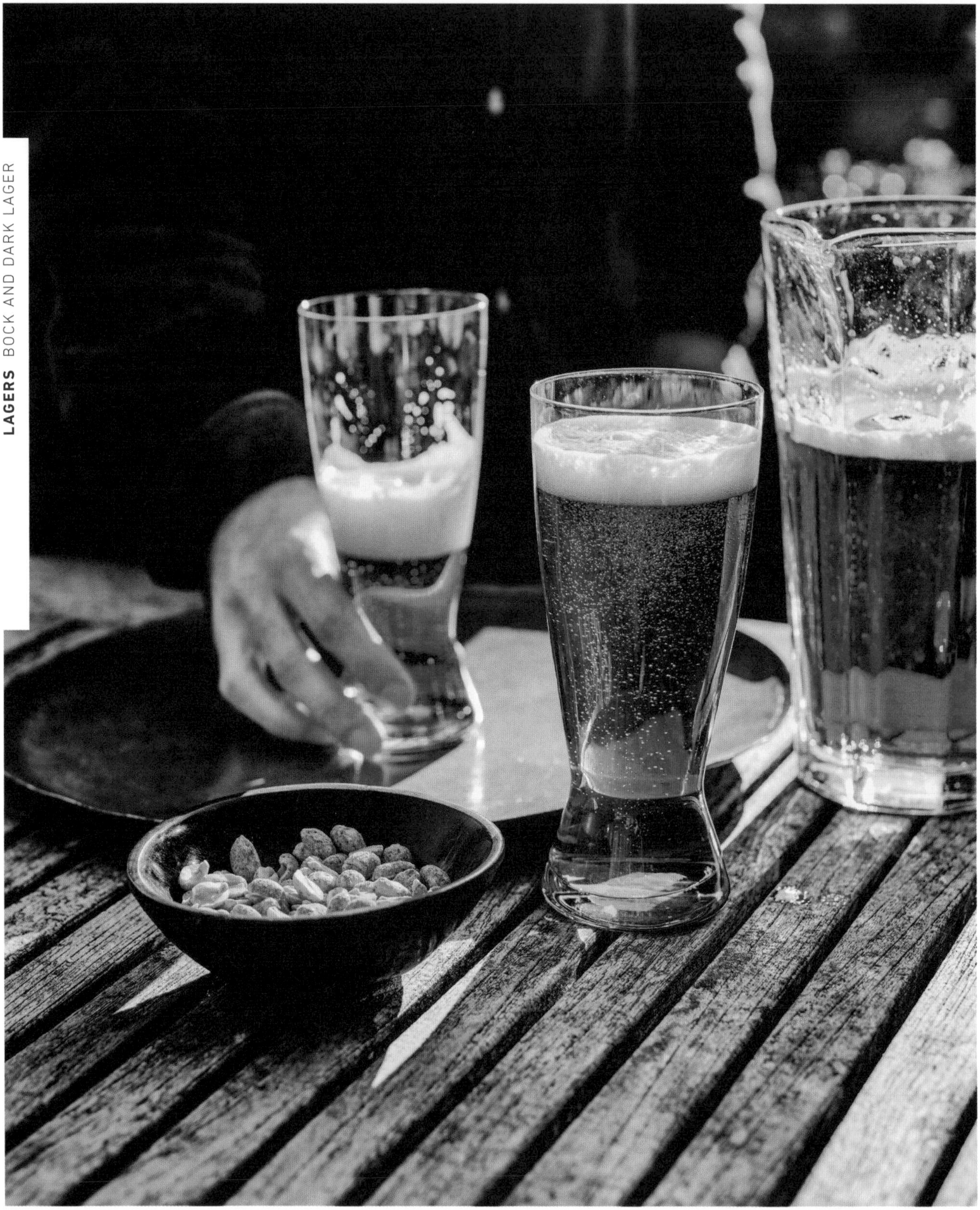

This delicious dark lager is lightly hopped with floral Hersbrucker and Perle hops. The end result is a smooth beer with a crisp finish.

DARK AMERICAN LAGER

ORIGINAL GRAVITY 1055 **EXPECTED FINAL GRAVITY** 1013 **TOTAL LIQUOR** 8.6 GALLONS (33 LITERS)

MAKES	READY TO DRINK	ESTIMATED ABV	BITTERNESS RATING	COLOR RATING
6 GALLONS (23 LITERS)	5 WEEKS	5.6%	19 IBU	31.9 EBC

FOR THE MASH

LIQUOR 3.6 gallons (14 liters) **MASH TIME** 1 hr **TEMPERATURE** 149°F (65°C)

Grain bill	Quantity
Pilsner malt	7lb 13oz (3.54kg)
Munich malt	1lb 11oz (766g)
Flaked corn (maize)	1lb 9oz (709g)
Special B	10½oz (300g)
Medium crystal malt	5⅓oz (153g)
Carafa special III malt	1¾oz (50g)

FOR THE BOIL

LIQUOR 7 gallons (27 liters) **BOIL TIME** 1 hr 15 mins

Hops	Quantity	IBU	When to add
Northern Brewer 8.0%	¾oz (22g)	18.9	At start of boil
Perle 8.0%	¼oz (6g)	0.2	For last 1 min of boil
Hallertauer Hersbrucker 3.5%	⅓oz (10g)	0.0	At end of boil

Other			
Irish moss	1 tsp		For last 15 mins of boil

TO FERMENT

FERMENTATION 54°F (12°C) **CONDITIONING** 4 weeks at 37°F (3°C)

Yeast
Wyeast 2124 Bohemian Lager

Hints of chocolate and caramel marry perfectly with the rich, malty sweetness of the Munich malt here. The result is a lager full of character with a classic, smooth finish.

MUNICH DUNKEL

ORIGINAL GRAVITY 1055 **EXPECTED FINAL GRAVITY** 1013 **TOTAL LIQUOR** 8.6 GALLONS (33 LITERS)

MAKES	READY TO DRINK	ESTIMATED ABV	BITTERNESS RATING	COLOR RATING
6 GALLONS (23 LITERS)	5 WEEKS	5.5%	27.4 IBU	34.4 EBC

FOR THE MASH

LIQUOR 3.6 gallons (14 liters) **MASH TIME** 1 hr **TEMPERATURE** 149°F (65°C)

Grain bill	Quantity
US domestic 2-row malt	4½lb (2kg)
Munich malt	6lb 10oz (3kg)
Biscuit malt	7oz (200g)
Chocolate wheat	3½oz (100g)
Carafa special II malt	2¾oz (80g)

FOR THE BOIL

LIQUOR 7 gallons (27 liters) **BOIL TIME** 1 hr 15 mins

Hops	Quantity	IBU	When to add
Magnum 11.0%	¾oz (23g)	26.9	At start of boil
Hallertauer Mittelfrüh 5.0%	¼oz (5g)	0.5	For last 5 mins of boil
Hallertauer Mittelfrüh 5.0%	⅓oz (9g)	0.0	At turn off
Other			
Irish moss	1 tsp		For last 15 mins of boil

TO FERMENT

FERMENTATION 54°F (12°C) **CONDITIONING** 4 weeks at 37°F (3°C)

Yeast
White Labs WLP830 German Lager

BREWER'S TIP

A triple decoction mash (see pp58–59) will give an enhanced maltiness to the beer and a greater depth of color.

As black as a stout but with a clean, refreshing, and light lager finish, this is a fantastic and unusual beer that will surprise and impress.

BLACK LAGER

ORIGINAL GRAVITY 1051 **EXPECTED FINAL GRAVITY** 1012 **TOTAL LIQUOR** 8.3 GALLONS (32 LITERS)

MAKES 6 GALLONS (23 LITERS)	READY TO DRINK 5 WEEKS	ESTIMATED ABV 5.1%	BITTERNESS RATING 38 IBU	COLOR RATING 57 EBC

FOR THE MASH

LIQUOR 3.4 gallons (13 liters)   **MASH TIME** 1 hr   **TEMPERATURE** 149°F (65°C)

Grain bill	Quantity
Pale malt	10lb (4.5kg)
Melanoidin malt	9oz (250g)
Chocolate malt	3½oz (100g)
Carafa special III malt	5½oz (150g)

FOR THE BOIL

LIQUOR 7 gallons (27 liters)   **BOIL TIME** 1 hr 15 mins

Hops	Quantity	IBU	When to add
Centennial 8.5%	1oz (32g)	28.5	At start of boil
Hallertauer Hersbrucker 3.5%	2oz (54g)	9.9	For last 15 mins of boil
Hallertauer Hersbrucker 3.5%	1½oz (46g)	0.0	At turn off

Other			
Irish moss	1 tsp		For last 15 mins of boil

TO FERMENT

FERMENTATION 57°F (14°C)   **CONDITIONING** 4 weeks at 37°F (3°C)

Yeast
White Labs WLP802 Czech Lager

MALT EXTRACT VERSION

Steep 9oz (250g) **melanoidin malt**, 3½oz (100g) **chocolate malt**, and 5½oz (150g) **Carafa special III malt** in 7 gallons (27 liters) water at 149°F (65°C) for 30 mins. Remove, then add 7lb 4oz (3.3kg) **dried extra-light malt extract**, bring to a boil, and add hops as specified in the main recipe.

ALES

A popular choice among home brewers, ale is quick and easy to produce since it can be brewed at room temperature and has a short conditioning period.

Ale is a full-flavored style of beer with a long history. In the Middle Ages, for example, it was a source of hydration and nutrition, with low-alcohol ales (known as "small beers") being consumed throughout the day due to the lack of fresh water.

TOP-FERMENTING YEAST

Modern ales are brewed at 61–72°F (16–22°C) using top-fermenting yeasts—yeasts that rise to the surface of the wort. These conditions allow the yeast to create lots of flavor compounds and esters, which can impart a wide range of complex fruit and malt flavors to the final brew.

MALTS AND HOPS

Most of the fermentable sugars in ale wort come from pale, malted barley, which is blended with darker malts for extra character. Hops are also used in all ales—in varying quantities. They provide bitterness, flavor, and aroma, help preserve the beer, and balance the taste of the alcohol. With a huge number of malt types and hop varieties available (see pp20–29), the possibilities for the adventurous home brewer are seemingly endless.

Ales are generally served cool, but not cold, to allow the malt and hop aromas to fully develop. Carbonation levels are typically low, and, for authenticity, ales are best stored in—and served from—a barrel or keg, rather than bottles.

Pale ale

Traditionally brewed with a large proportion of pale malts, and with soft water, pale ale has a smooth, balanced bitterness.

Appearance Pale straw to light golden with a small, lingering head.

Taste Smooth and creamy with subtle hop bitterness. Flavors from the yeast influence its character.

Aroma A light maltiness, with a hop aroma determined by the variety—English hops, for example, will impart subtle floral notes.

Strength 4–6% ABV

English pale ales have a light floral character and are not too bitter. There may be a slight butterscotch finish.

Belgian pale ales are strong, with spicy flavors from the Belgian yeast.

American pale ales have a very hoppy, citrus character and a clean, dry finish.

See pp104–115

India pale ale (IPA)

Created to withstand long sea journeys, IPA has high hop and alcohol levels.

Appearance Light straw to deep golden in color; good clarity with a thin, lingering head.

Taste Strong, spicy alcohol flavors with smooth bitterness and a dry finish.

Aroma Moderately hoppy; malt and caramel aromas are also common.

Strength 5–7.5% ABV

English IPAs have subtle floral and spicy hop aromas. Although they can have an assertive bitterness, this is usually well balanced by the alcohol content.

American IPAs have intense citrus hop aromas and flavors from the use of American hops. They are stronger than English IPAs, with an increased bitterness.

See pp121–136

Sour and lambic ales

The wild yeast used in these ales produces a sourness, often balanced by fruity or spicy notes.

Appearance Varies by style but often fruit-colored. Usually fairly hazy with a creamy head.

Taste Depends on the style but generally sweet, sour, sharp, and very distinct.

Aroma High fruit aromas, often with spicy notes.

Strength 3.2–7% ABV

Belgian varieties are typically high in alcohol, with the extended aging period creating a complex, flavorful beer akin to a fine red wine.

German varieties are sour, mildly fruity, highly carbonated, and have a very dry finish. They are low in alcohol and have a creamy, long-lasting head.

See pp137–139

Bitter

Often a commercial brewer's main beer, bitter has low carbonation levels and is best served from a cask via a hand pump.

Appearance Light gold to deep copper, with good clarity and a light head.

Taste More bitter than sweet but still perfectly balanced. Caramel or light fruit flavors are common.

Aroma Moderate to light hop aromas, with malt and sometimes caramel notes.

Strength 3.2–6% ABV

English bitters are lightly hopped, fairly low in strength, and have a sweetish finish with hints of fruit. Scottish bitters, which are fermented at lower temperatures, are cleaner and drier tasting.

See pp140–147

Strong ale

Often brewed for special occasions, strong ale is best enjoyed in moderation. Most will benefit from extended conditioning and aging.

Appearance Light copper to deep red, with a lasting off-white head. Sometimes slightly hazy.

Taste Varies by style but usually spicy and malty, often with fruit flavors from the fermentation process.

Aroma Little or no hop aroma, with malt and caramel characters.

Strength 6–9% ABV

English strong ales are often spiced with festive herbs and spices to create a delicious, complex beer. They are strong and deep amber in color.

Belgian strong ales, which are brewed all year round, are pale in color and have distinct spicy flavors and aromas from the unique yeast strains.

See pp148–157

Brown ale

A traditional English style that is becoming rare. Brown ale is mainly brewed in the north of England since demand has fallen elsewhere.

Appearance Dark amber to reddish brown, with an off-white head.

Taste Nutty with caramel and biscuit notes; a medium bitterness balances the sweetness.

Aroma Light hop aroma, with noticeable malts and caramel.

Strength 2.8–5.4% ABV

Northern English brown ales are strong, malty, and nutty, while those from the south are usually darker, sweeter, and lower in alcohol.

American brown ales are typically a bigger, maltier, hoppier interpretation of Northern English brown ales and often use citrusy American hops.

See pp160–163

Mild

A low-gravity, light-flavored beer created for drinking in quantity. Although becoming rare, mild is still popular in parts of England.

Appearance Deep copper to dark brown, with a light, short-lived head.

Taste Light with subtle hop flavors; surprisingly flavorful for the low alcohol content.

Aroma Little or no hop aroma, with caramel, biscuit, and roasted characters.

Strength 2.8–4.5% ABV

Traditionally, mild was popular in the English Midlands, where the refreshing and inexpensive brew was consumed by industrial workers.

See pp164–165

Barley wine

So called because it has the high strength and complex flavors often associated with wine, barley wine is particularly alchoholic.

Appearance Deep golden to dark amber. Due to the high alcohol content, it will leave legs, or streaks, on the glass when swirled.

Taste Sweet and complex malt flavors, including caramel, dried fruit, nut, and toffeelike notes.

Aroma Some hop aroma, with strong malt and caramel characters. Vintage versions are almost sherrylike.

Strength 8–12% ABV

English barley wines are intense with complex fruit and caramel flavors. A subtle bitterness and hop flavor balances the high alcohol content.

American barley wines have increased hop bitterness balanced with complex malt flavors and often citrusy notes.

See pp166–169

Porter

Originating in 18th-century London and descended from brown ale, porter was drunk by street and river porters—hence the name.

Appearance Dark brown or black.

Taste Mild roast flavors, a rich maltiness, and sometimes with hints of liquorice.

Aroma Roasted notes, with a slight chocolate character, maltiness, and a subtle smokiness.

Strength 4–7% ABV

Baltic porter—originally brewed in the Baltic states—is typically high in alcohol, with a sweet, malty character. It is often bottom fermented like a lager.

See pp170–173

Stout

Closely related to porter, stout was first known as "stout porter"—a stronger version of the style. It is full-bodied and very dark in color.

Appearance Very dark brown to jet-black. Often served with nitrogen to create a thick, creamy, tan head with no carbonation.

Taste Roasted and burnt bitter flavors; a smooth, creamy mouthfeel; low to moderate hop bitterness.

Aroma Roasted coffee aromas, sometimes with a chocolate-like character; low or no hop aroma.

Strength 4–7% ABV

Irish stout is the classic dry stout—with a famously thick and creamy head.

London stout has a lower gravity than other versions and can be quite sweet.

American stout has a strong hop bitterness and aroma.

See pp174–181

Zingy citrus flavors and aromas from the Galaxy
and Wai-ti hops help make this a particularly refreshing
beer with a balanced malty finish.

SPRING BEER

ORIGINAL GRAVITY 1046 **EXPECTED FINAL GRAVITY** 1012 **TOTAL LIQUOR** 8.2 GALLONS (31.5 LITERS)

MAKES 6 GALLONS (23 LITERS)	READY TO DRINK 5 WEEKS	ESTIMATED ABV 4.5%	BITTERNESS RATING 34.6 IBU	COLOR RATING 9.3 EBC

FOR THE MASH

LIQUOR 2.9 gallons (11.25 liters)   **MASH TIME** 1 hr   **TEMPERATURE** 149°F (65°C)

Grain bill	Quantity
Pale malt	8lb 13oz (4kg)
Munich malt	1lb 2oz (500g)

FOR THE BOIL

LIQUOR 7 gallons (27 liters)   **BOIL TIME** 1 hr 10 mins

Hops	Quantity	IBU	When to add
Galaxy 14.4%	1oz (30g)	34.6	At start of boil
Galaxy 14.4%	1oz (30g)	0.0	At end of boil
Wai-ti 4.5%	1oz (30g)	0.0	At end of boil

Other			
Irish moss	1 tsp		For last 15 mins of boil

TO FERMENT

FERMENTATION 64°F (18°C)   **CONDITIONING** 4 weeks at 54°F (12°C)

Yeast
Wyeast 1275 Thames Valley Ale

BREWER'S TIP

For an extra fruity aroma, try
dry hopping (see p61) with
scant 1oz (25g) Wai-ti hops
in the fermenter for 4 days.

Tawny colored and with a malty flavor, the dried elderflowers added to the boil give this ale a subtle yet unmistakably fruity finish, with a hint of peach.

ELDERFLOWER ALE

ORIGINAL GRAVITY 1045 EXPECTED FINAL GRAVITY 1011 TOTAL LIQUOR 8.2 GALLONS (31.5 LITERS)

MAKES 6 GALLONS (23 LITERS)	READY TO DRINK 5 WEEKS	ESTIMATED ABV 4.5%	BITTERNESS RATING 36.6 IBU	COLOR RATING 13.5 EBC

FOR THE MASH

LIQUOR 2.9 gallons (11.2 liters)   **MASH TIME** 1 hr   **TEMPERATURE** 149°F (65°C)

Grain bill	Quantity
Pale malt	9lb 8oz (4.3kg)
Medium crystal malt	3½oz (100g)
Chocolate malt	½oz (16g)

FOR THE BOIL

LIQUOR 7 gallons (27 liters)   **BOIL TIME** 1 hr 10 mins

Hops	Quantity	IBU	When to add
Challenger 7.0%	2oz (56g)	31.5	At start of boil
Dried elderflowers	½oz (15g)	0.0	For last 15 mins
Fuggle 4.5%	1oz (28g)	5.1	For last 10 mins
Challenger 7.0%	⅔oz (17g)	0.0	At end of boil

Other			
Irish moss	1 tsp		For last 15 mins of boil

TO FERMENT

FERMENTATION 68°F (20°C)   **CONDITIONING** 4 weeks at 54°F (12°C)

Yeast
Wyeast 1275 Thames Valley Ale

MALT EXTRACT VERSION

Steep 3½oz (100g) **medium crystal malt** and ½oz (16g) **chocolate malt** in 7 gallons (27 liters) water at 149°F (65°C) for 30 mins. Remove the malt, then add 6lb 1oz (2.75kg) **dried malt extract**, bring to a boil, and add the hops and elderflowers as specified in the main recipe.

This delightful pale ale celebrates the fall grain harvest and heralds the change of seasons. It is a fresh, crisp brew with a grainy flavor and citrus finish.

HARVEST PALE ALE

ORIGINAL GRAVITY 1041 **EXPECTED FINAL GRAVITY** 1010 **TOTAL LIQUOR** 8.2 GALLONS (31.5 LITERS)

MAKES	READY TO DRINK	ESTIMATED ABV	BITTERNESS RATING	COLOR RATING
6 GALLONS (23 LITERS)	5 WEEKS	4.2%	41 IBU	11 EBC

FOR THE MASH

LIQUOR 2.7 gallons (10.25 liters) **MASH TIME** 1 hr **TEMPERATURE** 149°F (65°C)

Grain bill	Quantity
US domestic 2-row malt	8lb 2oz (3.7kg)
Vienna malt	7oz (200g)
Crystal wheat malt	7oz (200g)

FOR THE BOIL

LIQUOR 7 gallons (27 liters) **BOIL TIME** 1 hr 10 mins

Hops	Quantity	IBU	When to add
Magnum 16%	¾oz (21g)	39.3	At start of boil
Willamette 6.3%	¼oz (7g)	1.8	For last 10 mins of boil
Willamette 6.3%	⅔oz (20g)	0.0	At end of boil
Cascade 6.6%	⅔oz (20g)	0.0	At end of boil

Other

Irish moss	1 tsp		For last 15 mins of boil

Yeast

White Labs WLP060 American Ale Yeast Blend

ESB, or "Extra Special Bitter," is traditionally brewed as a premium pale ale. Strong, malty, and with a slightly fruity, caramel finish, it is dangerously drinkable!

ESB ALE

ORIGINAL GRAVITY 1054 EXPECTED FINAL GRAVITY 1016 TOTAL LIQUOR 8.4 GALLONS (32.5 LITERS)

MAKES 6 GALLONS (23 LITERS)	READY TO DRINK 5 WEEKS	ESTIMATED ABV 5.1%	BITTERNESS RATING 32.5 IBU	COLOR RATING 16.2 EBC

FOR THE MASH

LIQUOR 3.5 gallons (13.5 liters)   **MASH TIME** 1 hr   **TEMPERATURE** 149°F (65°C)

Grain bill	Quantity
Pale malt	11lb (5kg)
Medium crystal malt	8oz (224g)
Torrified wheat	4oz (115g)
Chocolate malt	⅔oz (17g)

FOR THE BOIL

LIQUOR 7 gallons (27 liters)   **BOIL TIME** 1 hr 10 mins

Hops	Quantity	IBU	When to add
Challenger 7.0%	1¼oz (38g)	28.4	At start of boil
East Kent Golding 5.5%	⅔oz (20g)	4.1	For last 10 mins of boil
Fuggle 4.5%	½oz (13g)	0.0	At end of boil
Other			
Irish moss	1 tsp		For last 15 mins of boil

TO FERMENT

FERMENTATION 68°F (20°C)   **CONDITIONING** 4 weeks at 54°F (12°C)

Yeast
Wyeast 1187 Ringwood Ale

MALT EXTRACT VERSION

Steep 8oz (224g) **medium crystal malt** and ⅔oz (17g) **chocolate malt** in 7 gallons (27 liters) water at 149°F (65°C) for 30 mins. Remove the malt, then add 6lb 10oz (3kg) **dried malt extract** and 9oz (250g) **dried wheat malt extract**, bring to a boil, and add the hops as specified in the main recipe.

This page contains recipes for five separate single-hop ales.
The mash and fermentation stages are the same for each,
but select only one variety of hop to add during the boil.

SINGLE-HOP ALES

ORIGINAL GRAVITY 1050 **EXPECTED FINAL GRAVITY** 1012 **TOTAL LIQUOR** 8.5 GALLONS (32 LITERS)

MAKES	READY TO DRINK	ESTIMATED ABV	BITTERNESS RATING	COLOR RATING
6 GALLONS (23 LITERS)	7 WEEKS	5.9%	40 IBU	10 EBC

MASH

LIQUOR 3.2 gallons (12.3 liters) **MASH TIME** 1 hr **TEMPERATURE** 149°F (65°C)

Grain bill	Quantity
Pale malt	10lb 6oz (4.7kg)
Carapils malt	8¼oz (235g)

THE BOIL

LIQUOR 7 gallons (27 liters) **BOIL TIME** 1 hr 10 mins

AMARILLO
Pungent, with powerful citrus aromas

Hops	Quantity	IBU	When to add
Amarillo 5%	2oz (54g)	29.9	At start
Amarillo 5%	1oz (27g)	7.2	Last 15 mins
Amarillo 5%	1oz (27g)	2.9	Last 5 mins
Amarillo 5%	3oz (83g)	0.0	At end of boil

NELSON SAUVIN
Similar aroma to Sauvignon Blanc grapes, notes of gooseberry

Hops	Quantity	IBU	When to add
Nelson Sauvin 12.5%	¾oz (22g)	29.9	At start
Nelson Sauvin 12.5%	⅓oz (11g)	7.2	Last 15 mins
Nelson Sauvin 12.5%	⅓oz (11g)	2.9	Last 5 mins
Nelson Sauvin 12.5%	1¼oz (33g)	0.0	At end of boil

SAAZ
Floral and spicy character

Hops	Quantity	IBU	When to add
Saaz 4.2%	2¼oz (64g)	29.9	At start
Saaz 4.2%	1oz (32g)	7.2	Last 15 mins
Saaz 4.2%	1oz (32g)	2.9	Last 5 mins
Saaz 4.2%	3½oz (99g)	0.0	At end of boil

CASCADE
Floral and citrus quality, notes of grapefruit

Hops	Quantity	IBU	When to add
Cascade 6.6%	1½oz (41g)	29.9	At start
Cascade 6.6%	⅔oz (20g)	7.2	Last 15 mins
Cascade 6.6%	⅔oz (20g)	2.9	Last 5 mins
Cascade 6.6%	2¼oz (63g)	0.0	At end of boil

EAST KENT GOLDING
Subtle, floral, spicy aromas

Hops	Quantity	IBU	When to add
East Kent Golding 5.5%	1¾oz (49g)	29.9	At start
East Kent Golding 5.5%	¾oz (24g)	7.2	Last 15 mins
East Kent Golding 5.5%	¾oz (24g)	2.9	Last 5 mins
East Kent Golding 5.5%	2½oz (75g)	0.0	At end of boil

Other

Irish moss	1 tsp	For last 15 mins of boil

FERMENT

FERMENTATION 64°F (18°C) **CONDITIONING** 6 weeks at 54°F (12°C)

Yeast
Wyeast 1056 American Ale

MALT EXTRACT VERSION
Steep 10½oz (300g) **Carapils malt** in 7 gallons (27 liters) water at 149°F (65°C) for 30 mins. Remove the malt, then add 7lb 4oz (3.3kg) **dried wheat malt extract**, bring to a boil, and add your chosen hops as specified in the main recipe.

A golden-colored ale with a delicious floral aroma,

the low gravity of the wort—and low alcohol level

of the final brew—makes this a great session beer.

PALE ALE

ORIGINAL GRAVITY 1041 EXPECTED FINAL GRAVITY 1012 TOTAL LIQUOR 14.4 GALLONS (31.5 LITERS)

MAKES	READY TO DRINK	ESTIMATED ABV	BITTERNESS RATING	COLOR RATING
6 GALLONS (23 LITERS)	5 WEEKS	3.8%	26 IBU	7.1 EBC

FOR THE MASH

LIQUOR 2.9 gallons (11 liters) **MASH TIME** 1 hr **TEMPERATURE** 149°F (65°C)

Grain bill	Quantity
US domestic 2-row malt	9lb 8oz (4.3kg)
Light crystal malt	3⅓oz (95g)

FOR THE BOIL

LIQUOR 7 gallons (27 liters) **BOIL TIME** 1 hr 10 mins

Hops	Quantity	IBU	When to add
Challenger 7%	1¼oz (35g)	26	At start of boil
East Kent Golding 5.5%	¾oz (23g)	0.0	At end of boil
Styrian Golding 4.5%	½oz (16g)	0.0	At end of boil

Other			
Irish moss	1 tsp		For last 15 mins of boil

TO FERMENT

FERMENTATION 64°F (18°C) **CONDITIONING** 4 weeks at 54°F (12°C)

Yeast
White Labs WLP005 British Ale

MALT EXTRACT VERSION

Steep 3⅓oz (95g) **light crystal malt** in 7 gallons (27 liters) water at 149°F (65°C) for 30 mins. Remove the malt, then add 6lb 1oz (2.75kg) **dried extra-light malt extract**, bring to a boil, and add the hops as specified in the main recipe.

This delicious, strong, and refreshing ale has a crisp, dry finish. The honey imparts a dry rather than sweet flavor yet still gives the beer a distinct honey character.

HONEY ALE

ORIGINAL GRAVITY 1057 EXPECTED FINAL GRAVITY 1011 TOTAL LIQUOR 8.8 GALLONS (34 LITERS)

MAKES	READY TO DRINK	ESTIMATED ABV	BITTERNESS RATING	COLOR RATING
6 GALLONS (23 LITERS)	5 WEEKS	6.2%	10 IBU	16.2 EBC

FOR THE MASH

LIQUOR 3.2 gallons (12.5 liters) MASH TIME 1 hr TEMPERATURE 149°F (65°C)

Grain bill	Quantity
Pale malt	10lb (4.5kg)
Biscuit malt	12oz (350g)
Medium crystal malt	9oz (250g)

FOR THE BOIL

LIQUOR 7 gallons (27 liters) BOIL TIME 1 hr 15 mins

Hops	Quantity	IBU	When to add
Challenger 7%	½oz (12g)	9.6	At start of boil
Target 10.5%	¼oz (8g)	0.4	For last 1 min of boil

Other			
Irish moss	1 tsp		For last 15 mins of boil
Honey	1lb 2oz (500g)		For last 5 mins of boil

TO FERMENT

FERMENTATION 64°F (18°C) CONDITIONING 4 weeks at 54°F (12°C)

Yeast
Danstar Nottingham Dry Ale

MALT EXTRACT VERSION

Steep 12oz (350g) **biscuit malt** and 9oz (250g) **medium crystal malt** in 7 gallons (27 liters) water at 149°F (65°C) for 30 mins. Remove the malt, then add 6lb 4oz (2.85kg) **dried light malt extract**, bring to a boil, and add the hops as specified in the main recipe.

Traditionally known as "Fraoch," heather ale has been brewed in Scotland since 2000BCE. It is a lovely golden ale with an herbal, grassy aroma and slightly spicy finish.

HEATHER ALE

ORIGINAL GRAVITY 1051 **EXPECTED FINAL GRAVITY** 1014 **TOTAL LIQUOR** 8.4 GALLONS (32.5 LITERS)

MAKES 6 GALLONS (23 LITERS)	READY TO DRINK 5 WEEKS	ESTIMATED ABV 4.9%	BITTERNESS RATING 25 IBU	COLOR RATING 15.9 EBC

FOR THE MASH

LIQUOR 3.3 gallons (12.7 liters) **MASH TIME** 1 hr **TEMPERATURE** 149°F (65°C)

Grain bill	Quantity
Pale malt	9lb 9oz (4.34kg)
Caramalt	1lb 2oz (500g)
Crystal wheat malt	7oz (200g)

FOR THE BOIL

LIQUOR 7 gallons (27 liters) **BOIL TIME** 1 hr 10 mins

Hops	Quantity	IBU	When to add
Golding 5.5%	1½oz (41g)	2.5	At start of boil
Golding 5.5%	⅔oz (20g)	0.0	At end of boil

Other			
Fresh heather tips	2½oz (75g)		At start of boil
Irish moss	1 tsp		For last 15 mins of boil
Fresh heather tips	2½oz (75g)		At end of boil

TO FERMENT

FERMENTATION 64°F (18°C) **CONDITIONING** 4 weeks at 54°F (12°C)

Yeast
White Labs WLP028 Edinburgh Ale

MALT EXTRACT VERSION

Steep 1lb 2oz (500g) **Caramalt** and 7oz (200g) **crystal wheat malt** in 7 gallons (27 liters) water at 149°F (65°C) for 30 mins. Remove the malt, then add 6lb 3oz (2.8kg) **dried light malt extract**, bring to a boil, and add the hops as specified in the main recipe.

BREWER'S TIP

Try adding ⅔oz (20g) bog myrtle (a deciduous shrub also known as sweet gale) at the end of the boil to add a bittersweet, resinous character to the beer.

Lighter than its cousins Dubbel and Tripel (see pp156–157),
Belgian Pale Ale is an easy-drinking beer. The pale malts
and light hop varieties create a perfect flavor balance.

BELGIAN PALE ALE

ORIGINAL GRAVITY 1051   **EXPECTED FINAL GRAVITY** 1013   **TOTAL LIQUOR** 8.5 GALLONS (32.5 LITERS)

MAKES	READY TO DRINK	ESTIMATED ABV	BITTERNESS RATING	COLOR RATING
6 GALLONS (23 LITERS)	5 WEEKS	5.1%	25 IBU	16.7 EBC

FOR THE MASH

LIQUOR 3.3 gallons (12.8 liters)   **MASH TIME** 1 hr   **TEMPERATURE** 149°F (65°C)

Grain bill	Quantity
Belgian pale malt	10lb 2oz (4.6kg)
Caramunich I	1lb 2oz (500g)

FOR THE BOIL

LIQUOR 7 gallons (27 liters)   **BOIL TIME** 1 hr 10 mins

Hops	Quantity	IBU	When to add
Golding 5.5%	1¼oz (38g)	22.9	At start of boil
Saaz 4.2%	½oz (13g)	2.1	For last 10 mins of boil
Saaz 4.2%	1¼oz (38g)	0.0	At end of boil
Other			
Irish moss	1 tsp		For last 15 mins of boil

TO FERMENT

FERMENTATION 68°F (20°C)   **CONDITIONING** 4 weeks at 54°F (12°C)

Yeast
Wyeast 3522 Belgian Ardennes

MALT EXTRACT VERSION

Steep 1lb 2oz (500g) **Caramunich I malt** in 7 gallons
(27 liters) water at 149°F (65°C) for 30 mins. Remove
the malt, then add 6lb 6oz (2.9kg) **dried light malt
extract**, bring to a boil, and add the hops as specified in
the main recipe.

BREWER'S TIP

To produce a fruitier-flavored
beer, try changing the yeast to
Wyeast 3942 Belgian Wheat.

Originally brewed as a summer beer in the French-speaking region of Belgium, Saison is a refreshing, spicy ale with strong citrus notes.

SAISON

ORIGINAL GRAVITY 1051 **EXPECTED FINAL GRAVITY** 1010 **TOTAL LIQUOR** 8.3 GALLONS (32 LITERS)

MAKES	**READY TO DRINK**	**ESTIMATED ABV**	**BITTERNESS RATING**	**COLOR RATING**
6 GALLONS (23 LITERS)	5 WEEKS	5.6%	16 IBU	17.1 EBC

FOR THE MASH

LIQUOR 3.2 gallons (12.3 liters)   **MASH TIME** 1 hr   **TEMPERATURE** 149°F (65°C)

Grain bill	Quantity
Pilsner malt	7lb 14oz (3.57kg)
Munich malt	2lb (890g)
Wheat malt	6¼oz (180g)
Special B	4¾oz (135g)
Caramunich II	4¾oz (135g)

FOR THE BOIL

LIQUOR 7 gallons (27 liters)   **BOIL TIME** 1 hr 10 mins

Hops	Quantity	IBU	When to add
Magnum 11%	½oz (13g)	16.4	At start of boil
Styrian Golding Celeia 5.5%	⅔oz (20g)	0.0	At end of boil

Other		
Irish moss	1 tsp	For last 15 mins of boil
Honey	7oz (200g)	For last 5 mins of boil

TO FERMENT

FERMENTATION 75°F (24°C)
CONDITIONING 4 weeks at 54°F (12°C)

Yeast
Wyeast 3724 Belgian Saison

BREWER'S TIP

To ensure proper attenuation (conversion of sugar to alcohol), increase the fermentation temperature to 82°F (28°C) after 4 days.

Kveik farmhouse ales are traditionally brewed with water
that has been infused with juniper branches.
This is an easier version to make that is equally delicious.

KVEIK FARMHOUSE ALE

ORIGINAL GRAVITY 1050 **EXPECTED FINAL GRAVITY** 1008 **TOTAL LIQUOR** 8.6 GALLONS (32.5 LITERS)

MAKES 6 GALLONS (23 LITERS)	READY TO DRINK 3 WEEKS	ESTIMATED ABV 5.5%	BITTERNESS RATING 21 IBU	COLOR RATING 7.1 EBC

FOR THE MASH

LIQUOR 3.6 gallons (13.5 liters) **MASH TIME** 1 hr **TEMPERATURE** 149°F (65°C)

Grain bill	Quantity
Pilsner malt	8lb (4kg)
Wheat malt	1lb 2oz (500g)
Spelt malt	1lb 2oz (500g)
Carapils	14oz (400g)

FOR THE BOIL

LIQUOR 7 gallons (27 liters)   **BOIL TIME** 1 hr 15 mins

Hops	Quantity	IBU	When to add
Chinook 13.1%	¼oz (5g)	9.2	At start of boil
Chinook 13.1%	¼oz (5g)	7	For last 10 mins of boil
Chinook 13.1%	¼oz (5g)	4.9	At end of boil

Other			
Irish moss	1 tsp		For last 15 mins of boil
Spruce tips	1¾oz (50g)		For last 10 mins of boil
Spruce tips	1¾oz (50g)		At end of boil

TO FERMENT

FERMENTATION 68°F (20°C)   **CONDITIONING** 2 weeks at 50°F (10°C)

Yeast
Omega Yeast OYL061 Voss Kveik

BREWER'S TIP

Use fresh tips and possibly
small, cut-up twigs to add
more woody character.

In this brew, a light, smoky aroma from the beech-smoked
malt is complemented by citrus notes from
the hops and a clean finish from the yeast.

SMOKED BEER

ORIGINAL GRAVITY 1051 EXPECTED FINAL GRAVITY 1012 TOTAL LIQUOR 8.3 GALLONS (32 LITERS)

MAKES	READY TO DRINK	ESTIMATED ABV	BITTERNESS RATING	COLOR RATING
6 GALLONS (23 LITERS)	6 WEEKS	5.1%	30.2 IBU	23.6 EBC

FOR THE MASH

LIQUOR 3.3 gallons (12.7 liters) **MASH TIME** 1 hr **TEMPERATURE** 149°F (65°C)

Grain bill	Quantity
Pale malt	8lb 13oz (4kg)
Smoked malt	1lb 8oz (700g)
Medium crystal malt	10½oz (300g)
Carafa special II	2½oz (70g)

FOR THE BOIL

LIQUOR 7 gallons (27 liters) **BOIL TIME** 1 hr 10 mins

Hops	Quantity	IBU	When to add
Chinook 13.3%	⅔oz (18g)	25.9	At start of boil
Willamette 6.3%	⅔oz (18g)	4.3	For last 15 mins of boil
Willamette 6.3%	⅔oz (18g)	0.0	At end of boil

Other			
Irish moss	1 tsp		For last 15 mins of boil

TO FERMENT

FERMENTATION 64°F (18°C) **CONDITIONING** 4 weeks at 54°F (12°C)

Yeast
Wyeast 1056 American Ale

BREWER'S TIP

For an authentic barrel-aged
character, try adding
3½oz (100g) oak chips to
the fermenter after 3 days
and leave for 1 week
before removing.

Traditionally brewed by Belgian monks for personal consumption, Patersbier ("Father's Beer") is a simple, light, and surprisingly flavorful brew.

PATERSBIER

ORIGINAL GRAVITY 1046 EXPECTED FINAL GRAVITY 1010 TOTAL LIQUOR 8.2 GALLONS (31.5 LITERS)

MAKES 6 GALLONS (23 LITERS)	READY TO DRINK 4 WEEKS	ESTIMATED ABV 4.7%	BITTERNESS RATING 16.4 IBU	COLOR RATING 5.7 EBC

MASH

LIQUOR 2.9 gallons (11.25 liters) MASH TIME 1 hr TEMPERATURE 149°F (65°C)

Grain bill	Quantity
Belgian Pilsner malt	10lb (4.5kg)

FOR THE BOIL

LIQUOR 7 gallons (27 liters) BOIL TIME 1 hr 10 mins

Hops	Quantity	IBU	When to add
Saaz 4.2%	1oz (30g)	14.4	At start of boil
Hallertauer Mittelfrüh 5%	⅓oz (10g)	2.0	For last 10 mins of boil

Other			
Irish moss	1 tsp		For last 15 mins of boil

TO FERMENT

FERMENTATION 72°F (22°C) CONDITIONING 3 weeks at 54°F (12°C)

Yeast
Wyeast 3787 Trappist High Gravity

MALT EXTRACT VERSION
Add 6lb 6oz (2.9kg) **dried light malt extract** to 7 gallons (27 liters) water, bring to a boil, and add the hops as specified in the main recipe.

BREWER'S TIP

Try replacing the Hallertauer Mittelfrüh hops with more Saaz hops during the boil. This will give your brew a slightly more floral aroma.

This beer is super hazy, massively
dry-hopped, and has a soft, full mouthfeel—
it's like drinking fruit juice!

DOUBLE DRY HOPPED PALE ALE

ORIGINAL GRAVITY 1049 **EXPECTED FINAL GRAVITY** 1010 **TOTAL LIQUOR** 8.5 GALLONS (32 LITERS)

MAKES 6 GALLONS (23 LITERS)	READY TO DRINK 5 WEEKS	ESTIMATED ABV 5.2%	BITTERNESS RATING 29.6 IBU	COLOR RATING 7.5 EBC

FOR THE MASH

LIQUOR 3.4 gallons (13 liters)   **MASH TIME** 1 hr   **TEMPERATURE** 65°C (149°F)

Grain bill	Quantity
Pale malt	7lb (3.5kg)
Wheat malt	3lb 3oz (1.5kg)
Carapils malt	10oz (300g)

FOR THE BOIL

LIQUOR 3.4 gallons (13 liters)   **BOIL TIME** 1 hr 15 mins

Hops	Quantity	IBU	When to add
Simcoe 13.8%	1¾oz (50g)	17	At end of boil
Amarillo 10%	1¾oz (50g)	12.6	At end of boil

Other			
Irish moss	1 tsp		For last 15 mins of boil

TO FERMENT

FERMENTATION 64°F (18°C)   **CONDITIONING** 4 weeks at 39°F (4°C)

Yeast
Wyeast 1318 London Ale III

Hops	Quantity	When to add
Citra 13.8%	5½oz (150g)	For last 3 days 59°F (15°C)
Galaxy 14.5%	5½oz (150g)	For last 3 days 59°F (15°C)

BREWER'S TIP

For extra fruitiness, try adding
half of the dry hops earlier in
the fermentation—at a gravity
of around 1.020. Then add the
rest at final gravity.

First brewed in England in the 19th century for export,
the high alcohol content and hop levels in IPA (India Pale Ale)
helped preserve the beer on long sea voyages.

ENGLISH IPA

ORIGINAL GRAVITY 1060 **EXPECTED FINAL GRAVITY** 1017 **TOTAL LIQUOR** 8.6 GALLONS (33 LITERS)

MAKES	READY TO DRINK	ESTIMATED ABV	BITTERNESS RATING	COLOR RATING
6 GALLONS (23 LITERS)	5 WEEKS	5.7%	60.1 IBU	13 EBC

FOR THE MASH

LIQUOR 3.6 gallons (13.9 liters) **MASH TIME** 1 hr **TEMPERATURE** 149°F (65°C)

Grain bill	Quantity
Pale malt	12lb 9oz (5.8kg)
Crystal malt	5oz (145g)

FOR THE BOIL

LIQUOR 7 gallons (27 liters) **BOIL TIME** 1 hr 10 mins

Hops	Quantity	IBU	When to add
Challenger 7%	2½oz (70g)	50.5	At start of boil
Golding 5.5%	1¼oz (35g)	9.5	For last 15 mins of boil
Golding 5.5%	1¼oz (35g)	0.0	At end of boil

Other			
Irish moss	1 tsp		For last 15 mins of boil

TO FERMENT

FERMENTATION 64°F (18°C) **CONDITIONING** 4 weeks at 54°F (12°C)

Yeast
Wyeast 1187 Ringwood Ale

MALT EXTRACT VERSION

Steep 5oz (145g) **crystal malt** in 7 gallons (27 liters) water at 149°F (65°C) for 30 mins. Remove the malt, then add 8lb 2oz (3.7kg) **dried light malt extract**, bring to a boil, and add the hops as specified in the main recipe.

BREWER'S TIP

After 4 days, increase the temperature by 1.8°F (1°C) per day up to 72°F (22°C). This will help achieve the correct attenuation (conversion of sugar to alcohol).

121

This new and incredibly popular IPA style is characterized
by three things: a super soft bitterness; a hazy, thick,
creamy mouthfeel; and a massive dry hopping.

NEW ENGLAND IPA

ORIGINAL GRAVITY 1053 **EXPECTED FINAL GRAVITY** 1009 **TOTAL LIQUOR** 8.8 GALLONS (33.5 LITERS)

MAKES 6 GALLONS (23 LITERS)	READY TO DRINK 3 WEEKS	ESTIMATED ABV 5.9%	BITTERNESS RATING 29.9 IBU	COLOR RATING 8.3 EBC

FOR THE MASH

LIQUOR 3.8 gallons (14.5 liters)   **MASH TIME** 1 hr   **TEMPERATURE** 151°F (66°C)

Grain bill	Quantity		Grain bill	Quantity
Pilsner malt	8lb (4kg)		Vienna malt	1lb 2oz (500g)
Flaked oats	2¼lb (1kg)		Carapils	9oz (250g)

FOR THE BOIL

LIQUOR 7 gallons (27 liters)   **BOIL TIME** 1 hr 15 mins

Hops	Quantity	IBU	When to add
Simcoe 13.8%	1¾oz (50g)	17.3	At end of boil
Amarillo 10.1%	1¾oz (50g)	12.6	At end of boil

Other			
Irish moss	1 tsp		For last 15 mins of boil

TO FERMENT

FERMENTATION 68°F (20°C)   **CONDITIONING** 2 weeks at 50°F (10°C)

Yeast
Wyeast 1318 London Ale III

Hops	Quantity	When to add
Citra 13.8%	5½oz (150g)	For last 3 days
Galaxy 14.5%	3½oz (100g)	For last 3 days

BREWER'S TIP

This style will oxidize very
easily, so ensure that the
oxygen levels are kept to an
absolute minimum after
fermentation. Store cold
and drink fresh.

Multiple hoppings with three different hop varieties give this IPA a powerful, complex, yet well-balanced flavor and aroma—definitely one for the "hopheads."

60-MINUTE IPA

ORIGINAL GRAVITY 1055 EXPECTED FINAL GRAVITY 1013 TOTAL LIQUOR 8.6 GALLONS (33 LITERS)

MAKES 6 GALLONS (23 LITERS)	READY TO DRINK 7 WEEKS	ESTIMATED ABV 5.7%	BITTERNESS RATING 60 IBU	COLOR RATING 6.5 EBC

FOR THE MASH

LIQUOR 3.6 gallons (14 liters)   MASH TIME 1 hr   TEMPERATURE 149°F (65°C)

Grain bill	Quantity
Pale malt	12lb 2oz (5.5kg)

FOR THE BOIL

LIQUOR 7 gallons (27 liters)   BOIL TIME 1 hr

Hops	Quantity	IBU	When to add
Chinook 13.3%	¼oz (7g)	8.9	At start of boil
Amarillo 5.0%	¼oz (7g)	3.4	At start of boil
Chinook 13.3%	¼oz (7g)	6.9	For last 30 mins of boil
Amarillo 5.0%	¼oz (7g)	2.6	For last 30 mins of boil
Cascade 6.6%	¼oz (7g)	3.4	For last 30 mins of boil

Then ¼oz (7g) each of Chinook, Amarillo, and Cascade every 5 mins until 1 hr is up

Chinook 13.3%	⅓oz (10g)	0.0	At end of boil
Amarillo 5.0%	⅓oz (10g)	0.0	At end of boil
Cascade 6.6%	⅓oz (10g)	0.0	At end of boil

Other			
Irish moss	1 tsp		For last 15 mins of boil

TO FERMENT

FERMENTATION 64°F (18°C)   CONDITIONING 6 weeks at 54°F (12°C)

Yeast
White Labs WLP001 California Ale

MALT EXTRACT VERSION

Add 7lb 11oz (3.5kg) **dried extra-light malt extract** to 7 gallons (27 liters) water, bring to a boil, and add the hops as specified in the main recipe.

This brew has all the hallmarks of the classic American IPA—a hoppy bitterness, balanced by a relatively high alcohol content, and a powerful citrus aroma.

AMERICAN IPA

ORIGINAL GRAVITY 1060 **EXPECTED FINAL GRAVITY** 1014 **TOTAL LIQUOR** 8.8 GALLONS (34 LITERS)

MAKES	READY TO DRINK	ESTIMATED ABV	BITTERNESS RATING	COLOR RATING
6 GALLONS (23 LITERS)	7 WEEKS	6.2%	55 IBU	10.6 EBC

FOR THE MASH

LIQUOR 3.9 gallons (15 liters)   **MASH TIME** 1 hr   **TEMPERATURE** 149°F (65°C)

Grain bill	Quantity
Pale malt	13lb 4oz (6kg)

FOR THE BOIL

LIQUOR 7 gallons (27 liters)   **BOIL TIME** 1 hr 10 mins

Hops	Quantity	IBU	When to add
Citra 13.8%	1oz (29g)	40.9	At start of boil
Citra 13.8%	½oz (15g)	7.2	For last 10 mins of boil
Simcoe 13%	½oz (15g)	6.8	For last 10 mins of boil
Citra 13.8%	1½oz (44g)	0.0	At end of boil
Simcoe 13%	1½oz (44g)	0.0	At end of boil

Other			
Irish moss	1 tsp		For last 15 mins of boil

TO FERMENT

FERMENTATION 64°F (18°C)   **CONDITIONING** 6 weeks at 54°F (12°C)

Yeast
White Labs WLP060 American Ale Yeast Blend

Hops	Quantity	When to add
Citra 13.8%	1¾oz (50g)	After fermentation
Simcoe 13%	1¾oz (50g)	After fermentation

MALT EXTRACT VERSION
Add 8lb 4oz (3.75kg) **dried light malt extract** to 7 gallons (27 liters) water, bring to a boil, and add the hops as specified in the main recipe.

This beer is deceptively strong as the high levels of alcohol are balanced by a hop bitterness, sweet malt flavors, and a fresh, citrus aroma.

IMPERIAL IPA

ORIGINAL GRAVITY 1083 EXPECTED FINAL GRAVITY 1018 TOTAL LIQUOR 9.4 GALLONS (36 LITERS)

MAKES	READY TO DRINK	ESTIMATED ABV	BITTERNESS RATING	COLOR RATING
6 GALLONS (23 LITERS)	13 WEEKS	8.6%	75 IBU	24 EBC

FOR THE MASH

LIQUOR 5.5 gallons (21 liters) **MASH TIME** 1 hr **TEMPERATURE** 149°F (65°C)

Grain bill	Quantity
Pale malt	17lb 14oz (8.1kg)
Light crystal malt	3½oz (100g)
Chocolate malt	2¾oz (80g)

FOR THE BOIL

LIQUOR 7 gallons (27 liters) **BOIL TIME** 1 hr 10 mins

Hops	Quantity	IBU	When to add
Chinook 13.3%	2oz (56g)	64.0	At start of boil
Simcoe 13%	1oz (28g)	11.0	For last 10 mins of boil
Simcoe 13%	1¾oz (50g)	0.0	At end of boil
Willamette 6.3%	1¾oz (50g)	0.0	At end of boil

Other			
Irish moss	1 tsp		Fot last 15 mins of boil

TO FERMENT

FERMENTATION 68°F (20°C) **CONDITIONING** 12 weeks at 54°F (12°C)

Yeast
White Labs WLP001 California Ale

Hops	Quantity	IBU	When to add
Willamette 6.3%	1¾oz (50g)	0.0	Dry hop after 4 days

MALT EXTRACT VERSION

Steep 3½oz (100g) **light crystal malt** and 2¾oz (80g) **chocolate malt** in 7 gallons (27 liters) water at 149°F (65°C) for 30 mins. Remove the malt, then add 11lb 4oz (5.1kg) **dried light malt extract**, bring to a boil, and add the hops as specified in the main recipe.

As black as night but with the clean, citrus finish you would expect from a pale or golden ale, the contradiction in this beer will confuse the senses but delight the palate.

BLACK IPA

ORIGINAL GRAVITY 1054 **EXPECTED FINAL GRAVITY** 1018 **TOTAL LIQUOR** 8.6 GALLONS (33 LITERS)

MAKES 6 GALLONS (23 LITERS)	READY TO DRINK 7 WEEKS	ESTIMATED ABV 5.1%	ESTIMATED ABV 5.1%	COLOR RATING 56 EBC

FOR THE MASH

LIQUOR 3.5 gallons (13.5 liters)   **MASH TIME** 1 hr   **TEMPERATURE** 149°F (65°C)

Grain bill	Quantity
Pale malt	12lb 2oz (5.5kg)
Carafa special III	6oz (170g)
Chocolate malt	8oz (225g)

FOR THE BOIL

LIQUOR 7 gallons (27 liters)   **BOIL TIME** 1 hr 10 mins

Hops	Quantity	IBU	When to add
Apollo 19.5%	1oz (30g)	44.0	At start of boil
Citra 13.8%	1oz (30g)	16.0	For last 10 mins of boil
Amarillo 5%	1½oz (45g)	0.0	At end of boil
Citra 13.8%	1½oz (45g)	0.0	At end of boil

Other			
Irish moss	1 tsp		For last 15 mins of boil

TO FERMENT

FERMENTATION 64°F (18°C)   **CONDITIONING** 6 weeks at 54°F (12°C)

Yeast
Wyeast 1187 Ringwood Ale

Hops	Quantity	IBU	When to add
Citra 13.8%	1½oz (45g)	0.0	Dry hop after 4 days

MALT EXTRACT VERSION

Steep 6oz (170g) **Carafa special III malt** and 8oz (225g) **chocolate malt** in 7 gallons (27 liters) water at 149°F (65°C) for 30 mins. Remove the malt, then add 7lb (3.15kg) **dried malt extract**, bring to a boil, and add the hops as specified in the main recipe.

Fermented with 100 percent Brettanomyces yeast,
this IPA has wonderful complexity that changes as it ages.
Try different strains of brett for a variety of interesting characters.

BRETT IPA

ORIGINAL GRAVITY 1051 **EXPECTED FINAL GRAVITY** 1007 **TOTAL LIQUOR** 8.7 GALLONS (32.75 LITERS)

MAKES 6 GALLONS (23 LITERS)	READY TO DRINK 5 WEEKS	ESTIMATED ABV 5.7%	BITTERNESS RATING 35.5 IBU	COLOR RATING 7.7 EBC

FOR THE MASH

LIQUOR 3.6 gallons (13.75 liters) **MASH TIME** 1 hr **TEMPERATURE** 151°F (66°C)

Grain bill	Quantity
Pale malt	8lb (4kg)
Wheat malt	2¾lb (1.25kg)
Caramalt	9oz (250g)

FOR THE BOIL

LIQUOR 7 gallons (27 liters) **BOIL TIME** 1 hr 15 mins

Hops	Quantity	IBU	When to add
Citra 13.8%	¼oz (10g)	4	Last 10 mins of boil
Amarillo 10.1%	¼oz (10g)	2.7	Last 10 mins of boil
Citra 13.8%	1¾oz (50g)	17.2	At end of boil
Amarillo 10.1%	1¾oz (50g)	11.6	At end of boil

Other		
Irish moss	1 tsp	For last 15 mins of boil

TO FERMENT

FERMENTATION 68°F (20°C) **CONDITIONING** 4 weeks at 39°F (4°C)

Yeast
Yeast Bay WLP4637—Amalgamation—Brett Super Blend

Hops	Quantity	IBU	When to add
Citra 13.8%	1¾oz (50g)		Last 3 days 59°F (15°C)
Amarillo 10.1%	1¾oz (50g)		Last 3 days 59°F (15°C)
Chinook 13.1%	1¾oz (50g)		Last 3 days 59°F (15°C)

This extra-dry IPA originates from the San Francisco area. The enzyme added at the end of fermentation breaks down the beer's sugars, making it easier for the yeast to consume them. This gives the Brut IPA its dry character.

BRUT IPA

ORIGINAL GRAVITY 1044 **EXPECTED FINAL GRAVITY** 1000 OR BELOW **TOTAL LIQUOR** 8.2 GALLONS (31 LITERS)

MAKES 6 GALLONS (23 LITERS)	READY TO DRINK 5 WEEKS	ESTIMATED ABV 5.8%	BITTERNESS RATING 35.3 IBU	COLOR RATING 5.7 EBC

FOR THE MASH

LIQUOR 3.2 gallons (12 liters)   **MASH TIME** 1 hr   **TEMPERATURE** 145°F (63°C)

Grain bill	Quantity
Pilsner malt	8lb (4kg)
Wheat malt	1lb 2oz (500g)
Carapils malt	9oz (250g)

FOR THE BOIL

LIQUOR 3.2 gallons (12 liters)   **BOIL TIME** 1 hr 15 mins

Hops	Quantity	IBU	When to add
Magnum 16%	¼oz (10g)	20.2	At start of boil
Citra 13.8%	1oz (25g)	7.9	At end of boil
Nelson Sauvin 12.6%	1oz (25g)	7.2	At end of boil

Other			
Irish moss	1 tsp		For last 15 mins of boil

TO FERMENT

FERMENTATION 64°F (18°C)   **CONDITIONING** 4 weeks at 39°F (4°C)

Yeast
White Labs WLP007 Dry English Ale

Hops	Quantity	When to add
Citra 13.8%	1¾oz (50g)	After fermentation for 3 days
Nelson Sauvin 12.6%	1¾oz (50g)	After fermentation for 3 days
Sorachi Ace 14.9%	1¾oz (25g)	After fermentation for 3 days

Other		
Amylase (dry beer) enzyme		At 1.020 gravity

Sweet, soft malt and lactose flavors merge with citrus character from the fruit and hops.

MILKSHAKE IPA

ORIGINAL GRAVITY 1075 **EXPECTED FINAL GRAVITY** 1019 **TOTAL LIQUOR** 9.5 GALLONS (36 LITERS)

MAKES 6 GALLONS (23 LITERS)	READY TO DRINK 3 WEEKS	ESTIMATED ABV 7.5%	BITTERNESS RATING 25 IBU	COLOR RATING 8.9 EBC

FOR THE MASH

LIQUOR 4.5 gallons (17 liters) **MASH TIME** 1 hr **TEMPERATURE** 151°F (66°C)

Grain bill	Quantity	Grain bill	Quantity
Pilsner malt	9½lb (4.7kg)	Carapils malt	14oz (400g)
Wheat malt	2¼lb (1kg)	Flaked oats	14oz (400g)
Vienna malt	14oz (400g)		

FOR THE BOIL

LIQUOR 7 gallons (27 liters) **BOIL TIME** 1 hr 15 mins

Hops	Quantity	IBU	When to add
Cascade 6.1%	1oz (25g)	10.0	At end of boil
Amarillo 10.1%	1oz (25g)	15.0	At end of boil

Other			
Irish moss	1 tsp		For last 15 mins of boil
Lactose	2¼lb (1kg)		For last 10 mins of boil
Lemongrass	¾oz (20g)		For last 10 mins of boil

TO FERMENT

FERMENTATION 68°F (20°C) **CONDITIONING** 2 weeks at 50°F (10°C)

Yeast
Wyeast 1318 London Ale III

Hops	Quantity	When to add
Citra 13.8%	1¾oz (50g)	For last 3 days of fermentation
Simcoe 13.8%	1¾oz (50g)	For last 3 days of fermentation
Mosaic 12%	1¾oz (50g)	For last 3 days of fermentation

Other		
Peach puree	1lb 2oz (500g)	At 1.020 gravity
Vanilla beans	2	For last 3 days of fermentation

The soft, sweet vanilla in this IPA gives it
a rich mouthfeel and body, complementing the woodiness
of the rosemary and Chinook hops.

ROSEMARY AND VANILLA IPA

ORIGINAL GRAVITY 1050 **EXPECTED FINAL GRAVITY** 1013 **TOTAL LIQUOR** 8.5 GALLONS (32 LITERS)

MAKES	READY TO DRINK	ESTIMATED ABV	BITTERNESS RATING	COLOR RATING
6 GALLONS (23 LITERS)	3 WEEKS	4.9%	42.4 IBU	7.2 EBC

FOR THE MASH

LIQUOR 3.4 gallons (13 liters) **MASH TIME** 1 hr **TEMPERATURE** 153°F (67°C)

Grain bill	Quantity
Pilsner malt	17lb 14oz (8.1kg)
Wheat malt	1lb 2oz (500g)
Carapils malt	14oz (400g)

FOR THE BOIL

LIQUOR 7 gallons (27 liters) **BOIL TIME** 1 hr 15 mins

Hops	Quantity	IBU	When to add
Chinook 18.4%	¼oz (10g)	18.4	At start of boil
Chinook 13.1%	¼oz (10g)	14.0	For last 10 mins of boil
Chinook 13.1%	¼oz (10g)	10.0	At end of boil
Other			
Rosemary	1¾oz (50g)		For last 10 mins of boil
Irish moss	1 tsp		For last 15 mins of boil

TO FERMENT

FERMENTATION 95°F (35°C) **CONDITIONING** 2 weeks at 50°F (10°C)

Yeast
Wyeast 3944 Belgian Witbier

Hops	Quantity	When to add
Citra 13.8%	1¾oz (50g)	After fermentation
Other		
Rosemary	1¾oz (50g)	After fermentation
Vanilla beans	2	After fermentation

A delicious, softly fruited beer that appeals to
beer lovers and non-beer lovers alike.

PEACH IPA

ORIGINAL GRAVITY 1045 **EXPECTED FINAL GRAVITY** 1012 **TOTAL LIQUOR** 8.2 GALLONS (31 LITERS)

MAKES	READY TO	ESTIMATED	BITTERNESS	COLOR
6 GALLONS	DRINK	ABV	RATING	RATING
(23 LITERS)	5 WEEKS	4.9%	17 IBU	6.7 EBC

FOR THE MASH

LIQUOR 3.2 gallons (12 liters) **MASH TIME** 1 hr **TEMPERATURE** 151°F (66°C)

Grain bill	Quantity
Pilsner malt	8lb (4kg)
Wheat malt	1lb 2oz (500g)
Carapils malt	10oz (300g)

FOR THE BOIL

LIQUOR 7 gallons (27 liters) **BOIL TIME** 1 hr 15 mins

Hops	Quantity	IBU	When to add
Simcoe 13.8%	1¾oz (50g)	17	At end of boil

Other			
Irish moss	1 tsp		For last 15 mins of boil

TO FERMENT

FERMENTATION 64°F (18°C) **CONDITIONING** 4 weeks at 39°F (4°C)

Yeast
Wyeast 1318 London Ale III

Hops	Quantity	When to add
Citra 13.8%	1¾oz (50g)	For last 3 days of fermentation
Simcoe 13.8%	1¾oz (50g)	For last 3 days of fermentation

MALT EXTRACT VERSION

Steep **carapils malt** in 7 gallons (27 liters) water at 149°F (65°C) for 30 mins. Remove, then add 4½lb (2kg) **dried light malt extract** and 2¼lb (1kg) **dried wheat malt extract**, bring to a boil, and add the hops as specified in the main recipe.

Delicious, refreshing, and cloudy, this IPA
has a beautiful pink color and is delicately
flavored with rose petals and hibiscus.

WHITE IPA WITH ROSE AND HIBISCUS

ORIGINAL GRAVITY 1041 **EXPECTED FINAL GRAVITY** 1009 **TOTAL LIQUOR** 7.5 GALLONS (28.5 LITERS)

MAKES 6 GALLONS (23 LITERS)	READY TO DRINK 3 WEEKS	ESTIMATED ABV 4.2%	BITTERNESS RATING 36.2 IBU	COLOR RATING 7.7 EBC

FOR THE MASH

LIQUOR 2.5 gallons (9.5 liters) **MASH TIME** 1 hr **TEMPERATURE** 149°F (65°C)

Grain bill	Quantity
Pilsner malt	5½lb (2.5kg)
Wheat malt	3lb 12oz (1.7kg)
Caramalt	9oz (250g)

FOR THE BOIL

LIQUOR 7 gallons (27 liters) **BOIL TIME** 1 hr 15 mins

Hops	Quantity	IBU	When to add
Cascade 6.1%	¼oz (10g)	6.5	For last 10 mins of boil
Citra 13.8%	¼oz (10g)	14.7	For last 10 mins of boil
Cascade 6.1%	¼oz (10g)	4.6	At end of boil
Citra 13.8%	¼oz (10g)	10.4	At end of boil

Other			
Irish moss	1 tsp		For last 15 mins of boil
Dried hibiscus	1oz (25g)		At end of boil

TO FERMENT

FERMENTATION 95°F (35°C) **CONDITIONING** 2 weeks at 50°F (10°C)

Yeast
Wyeast 3944 Belgian Witbier

Hops	Quantity	When to add
Citra 13.8%	1¾oz (50g)	After fermentation for 3 days

A long aging process is needed to fully develop
the flavors in this complex, sour, and fruity beer—once bottled,
wait for at least a year before sampling.

FLANDERS RED ALE

ORIGINAL GRAVITY 1056 **EXPECTED FINAL GRAVITY** 1010 **TOTAL LIQUOR** 8.7 GALLONS (33 LITERS)

MAKES 6 GALLONS (23 LITERS)	READY TO DRINK 1+ YEARS	ESTIMATED ABV 6.2%	BITTERNESS RATING 20.7 IBU	COLOR RATING 29 EBC

FOR THE MASH

LIQUOR 3.7 gallons (14 liters)   **MASH TIME** 1 hr   **TEMPERATURE** 149°F (65°C)

Grain bill	Quantity
Vienna malt	7lb 1oz (3.2kg)
Pale malt	3lb 8oz (1.6kg)
Wheat malt	9oz (250g)
Special B	10½oz (300g)
Caramunich III	10½oz (300g)

FOR THE BOIL

LIQUOR 7 gallons (27 liters)   **BOIL TIME** 1 hr 10 mins

Hops	Quantity	IBU	When to add
East Kent Golding 5.5%	1¼oz (36g)	20.7	At start of boil

Other			
Irish moss	1 tsp		For last 15 mins of boil

TO FERMENT

FERMENTATION at least 4 weeks at 72°F (22°C)   **CONDITIONING** at least
6 months at 72°F (22°C)

Yeast
Wyeast 3763 Roeselare Ale Blend

BREWER'S TIP

Try adding a little fresh fruit
to the conditioning fermenter
after 3 months. Cherries or
raspberries are a good choice.

Delicate green tea, zingy, tart sourness, and soft,
sweet peach flavors combine into a refreshing, unique beer.
For detailed instructions about kettle souring, see pp66–67.

PEACH AND GREEN TEA KETTLE SOUR

ORIGINAL GRAVITY 1044 **EXPECTED FINAL GRAVITY** 1007 **TOTAL LIQUOR** 8.2 GALLONS (31 LITERS)

MAKES	READY TO DRINK	ESTIMATED ABV	BITTERNESS RATING	COLOR RATING
6 GALLONS (23 LITERS)	3 WEEKS	4.8%	0 IBU	6.5 EBC

FOR THE MASH

LIQUOR 3.2 gallons (12 liters)   **MASH TIME** 1 hr   **TEMPERATURE** 153°F (67°C)

Grain bill	Quantity	When to add
Pilsner malt	6½lb (3 kg)	
Wheat malt	3lb 3oz (1.5kg)	
Carapils malt	9oz (250g)	

Kettle sour		
Lactobacillus	95°F (35°C)	After sparge, for 24 hrs or until wort is pH3.4.

FOR THE BOIL

LIQUOR 7 gallons (27 liters)   **BOIL TIME** 1 hr 15 mins

Other	Quantity	When to add
Irish moss	1 tsp	For last 15 mins of boil

TO FERMENT

FERMENTATION 68°F (20°C)   **CONDITIONING** 2 weeks at 50°F (10°C)

Yeast
Wyeast 1318 London Ale III

Other	Quantity	When to add
Peach puree	7oz (200g)	After fermentation
Green tea	3½oz (100g)	After fermentation

Let the beer rest until the gravity is stable.

Lambic is a traditional Belgian style of sour beer. Most of the flavor profiles come from the wild yeast strains, which are added after primary fermentation.

CHERRY LAMBIC

ORIGINAL GRAVITY 1060 **EXPECTED FINAL GRAVITY** 1005 **TOTAL LIQUOR** 8.8 GALLONS (34 LITERS)

MAKES	READY TO DRINK	ESTIMATED ABV	BITTERNESS RATING	COLOR RATING
6 GALLONS (23 LITERS)	10 WEEKS	7.3%	15 IBU	10 EBC

FOR THE MASH

LIQUOR 4.6 gallons (17.5 liters) **MASH TIME** 1 hr **TEMPERATURE** 149°F (65°C)

Grain bill	Quantity
Pale malt	10lb (4.5kg)
Wheat malt	3lb 3oz (1.5kg)

FOR THE BOIL

LIQUOR 7 gallons (27 liters) **BOIL TIME** 1 hr 10 mins

Hops	Quantity	IBU	When to add
Challenger 13.3%	1oz (30g)	14.0	At start of boil

Other			
Irish moss	1 tsp		For last 15 mins of boil

TO FERMENT

FERMENTATION 72°F (22°C) for 2 weeks, then add secondary yeast strains and ferment for another 4 weeks **CONDITIONING** 4 weeks at 54°F (12°C)

Yeast
Safbrew WB-06, along with 13lb 4oz (6kg) morello cherries

After 2 weeks, add Wyeast 5335 Lactobacillus, Wyeast 5526 Brettanomyces Lambicus, and Wyeast 5733 Pediococcus and leave for another 4 weeks

MALT EXTRACT VERSION
Add 4½lb (2kg) **dried light malt extract** and 3lb 12oz (1.7kg) **dried wheat malt extract** to 7 gallons (27 liters) water, bring to a boil, and add the hops as specified in the main recipe.

BREWER'S TIP

Use a separate, dedicated fermenter for this brew since the wild yeast strains may contaminate future batches of beer.

This tawny-colored classic English bitter achieves a perfect balance between malt and hops. The London yeast creates an addictive, sweet, and slightly fruity finish.

LONDON BITTER

ORIGINAL GRAVITY 1044 **EXPECTED FINAL GRAVITY** 1012 **TOTAL LIQUOR** 8.3 GALLONS (32 LITERS)

MAKES	READY TO DRINK	ESTIMATED ABV	BITTERNESS RATING	COLOR RATING
6 GALLONS (23 LITERS)	5 WEEKS	4.3%	22.1 IBU	17 EBC

FOR THE MASH

LIQUOR 2.9 gallons (11 liters)   **MASH TIME** 1 hr   **TEMPERATURE** 149°F (65°C)

Grain bill	Quantity
Pale malt	8lb 13oz (4kg)
Medium crystal malt	14oz (396g)

FOR THE BOIL

LIQUOR 7 gallons (27 liters)   **BOIL TIME** 1 hr 10 mins

Hops	Quantity	IBU	When to add
Challenger 7.0%	1oz (25g)	20.3	At start of boil
Fuggle 4.5%	⅓oz (10g)	1.8	For last 10 mins of boil
Golding 5.5%	¼oz (6g)	0.0	At end of boil

Other			
Irish moss	1 tsp		For last 15 mins of boil

TO FERMENT

FERMENTATION 64°F (18°C)   **CONDITIONING** 4 weeks at 54°F (12°C)

Yeast
Wyeast 1318 London Ale III

MALT EXTRACT VERSION

Steep 14oz (396g) **medium crystal malt** in 7 gallons (27 liters) water at 149°F (65°C) for 30 mins. Remove the malt, then add 5½lb (2.5kg) **dried malt extract**, bring to a boil, and add the hops as specified in the main recipe.

BREWER'S TIP

For a less sweet beer, try using just 7oz (200g) crystal malt in the mash and add 1oz (30g) chocolate malt.

A full-bodied amber beer with a subtle chocolate flavor
that develops into a pithy bitterness, Yorkshire Bitter is traditionally
served with a creamy white head.

YORKSHIRE BITTER

ORIGINAL GRAVITY 1041 **EXPECTED FINAL GRAVITY** 1012 **TOTAL LIQUOR** 8.2 GALLONS (31.5 LITERS)

MAKES	READY TO	ESTIMATED	BITTERNESS	COLOR
6 GALLONS	DRINK	ABV	RATING	RATING
(23 LITERS)	5 WEEKS	3.8%	31 IBU	18 EBC

FOR THE MASH

LIQUOR 2.7 gallons (10.5 liters) **MASH TIME** 1 hr **TEMPERATURE** 149°F (65°C)

Grain bill	Quantity
Pale malt	7lb 11oz (3.5kg)
Medium crystal malt	7oz (200g)
Torrified wheat	12oz (350g)
Chocolate malt	1½oz (42g)

FOR THE BOIL

LIQUOR 7 gallons (27 liters) **BOIL TIME** 1 hr 10 mins

Hops	Quantity	IBU	When to add
Challenger 7.0%	1oz (29g)	24.3	At start of boil
First Gold 8.0%	⅔oz (20g)	6.7	For last 10 mins of boil
First Gold 8.0%	½oz (12g)	0.0	At end of boil

Other			
Irish moss	1 tsp		For last 15 mins of boil

TO FERMENT

FERMENTATION 68°F (20°C) **CONDITIONING** 4 weeks at 54°F (12°C)

Yeast
Wyeast 1469 West Yorkshire Ale

MALT EXTRACT VERSION

Steep 7oz (200g) **medium crystal malt** and 1½oz (42g)
chocolate malt in 7 gallons (27 liters) water at 149°F (65°C)
for 30 mins. Remove the malt, then add 4½lb (2kg) **dried malt
extract** and 1lb (450g) **dried wheat malt extract**, bring to a
boil, and add the hops as specified in the main recipe.

BREWER'S TIP

Serve from a cask using
a beer engine (pump)
and a swan-neck adapter
fitted with a sparklet—this
will aerate the beer and
produce a creamy head.

A delicious and light session beer for those long summer evenings. Although low in gravity, this ale is packed with flavor and has a wonderful hoppy finish.

SUMMER ALE

ORIGINAL GRAVITY 1038 **EXPECTED FINAL GRAVITY** 1012 **TOTAL LIQUOR** 8.1 GALLONS (31 LITERS)

MAKES 6 GALLONS (23 LITERS)	READY TO DRINK 5 WEEKS	ESTIMATED ABV 3.8%	BITTERNESS RATING 29.3 IBU	COLOR RATING 13 EBC

FOR THE MASH

LIQUOR 2.5 gallons (9.5 liters) **MASH TIME** 1 hr **TEMPERATURE** 149°F (65°C)

Grain bill	Quantity
Pale malt	7½lb (3.4kg)
Medium crystal malt	10½oz (300g)

FOR THE BOIL

LIQUOR 7 gallons (27 liters) **BOIL TIME** 1 hr 10 mins

Hops	Quantity	IBU	When to add
East Kent Golding 5.5%	⅔oz (20g)	9.4	At start of boil
Progress 5.5%	½oz (15g)	7.0	At start of boil
East Kent Golding 5.5%	½oz (15g)	7.5	For last 30 mins of boil
Progress 5.5%	⅓oz (10g)	5.0	For last 30 mins of boil
East Kent Golding 5.5%	½oz (15g)	0.4	For last 1 min of boil

Other			
Irish moss	1 tsp		For last 15 mins of boil

TO FERMENT

FERMENTATION 68°F (20°C) **CONDITIONING** 4 weeks at 54°F (12°C)

Yeast
Wyeast 1098 British Ale

MALT EXTRACT VERSION

Steep 10½oz (300g) **medium crystal malt** in 7 gallons (27 liters) water at 149°F (65°C) for 30 mins. Remove the malt, then add 4lb 13oz (2.2kg) **dried malt extract**, bring to a boil, and add the hops as specified in the main recipe.

BREWER'S TIP

Store in a barrel, rather than in bottles, and serve with a minimum amount of head for a light, hoppy, easy-drinking pint.

Strong and malty with biscuity undertones and notes
of black currant, this is a delicious and satisfying brew
to be savored after a long day at work.

CORNISH TIN MINER'S ALE

ORIGINAL GRAVITY 1058 **EXPECTED FINAL GRAVITY** 1019 **TOTAL LIQUOR** 8.6 GALLONS (33 LITERS)

MAKES	READY TO DRINK	ESTIMATED ABV	BITTERNESS RATING	COLOR RATING
6 GALLONS (23 LITERS)	9 WEEKS	5.2%	39.9 IBU	19 EBC

FOR THE MASH

LIQUOR 3.8 gallons (14.5 liters)   **MASH TIME** 1 hr   **TEMPERATURE** 149°F (65°C)

Grain bill	Quantity
Pale malt	10lb 13oz (4.9kg)
Caramunich	13½oz (380g)
Biscuit malt	9oz (250g)
Medium crystal malt	6½oz (185g)

FOR THE BOIL

LIQUOR 7 gallons (27 liters)   **BOIL TIME** 1 hr 10 mins

Hops	Quantity	IBU	When to add
First Gold 8%	1½oz (46g)	38.0	At start of boil
Bramling Cross 6%	½oz (15g)	3.3	For last 10 mins of boil
Bramling Cross 6%	½oz (15g)	0.0	At end of boil

Other			
Irish moss	1 tsp		For last 15 mins of boil

TO FERMENT

FERMENTATION 68°F (20°C)   **CONDITIONING** 8 weeks at 54°F (12°C)

Yeast
White Labs WLP002 English Ale

MALT EXTRACT VERSION

Steep 13½oz (380g) **Caramunich**, 9oz (250g) **biscuit malt**, and 6½oz (185g) **medium crystal malt** in 7 gallons (27 liters) water at 149°F (65°C) for 30 mins. Remove the malt, then add 7lb (3.15kg) **dried extra light malt extract**, bring to a boil, and add the hops as specified in the main recipe.

BREWER'S TIP

Try changing the yeast to White Labs WLP007 Dry English Ale for a drier-flavored version of this brew.

Closely related in style to English bitter, Irish Red Ale is a refreshing, lightly hopped beer with a malty flavor, clean finish, and distinctive red hue.

IRISH RED ALE

ORIGINAL GRAVITY 1051 **EXPECTED FINAL GRAVITY** 1013 **TOTAL LIQUOR** 8.4 GALLONS (32.5 LITERS)

MAKES 6 GALLONS (23 LITERS)	READY TO DRINK 7 WEEKS	ESTIMATED ABV 5.0%	BITTERNESS RATING 24.5 IBU	COLOR RATING 23 EBC

FOR THE MASH

LIQUOR 3.3 gallons (12.8 liters)   **MASH TIME** 1 hr   **TEMPERATURE** 149°F (65°C)

Grain bill	Quantity
Pale malt	10lb 2oz (4.6kg)
Medium crystal malt	7oz (200g)
Flaked barley	10½oz (300g)
Roasted barley	1¾oz (50g)

FOR THE BOIL

LIQUOR 7 gallons (27 liters)   **BOIL TIME** 1 hr 10 mins

Hops	Quantity	IBU	When to add
Fuggle 4.5%	1¾oz (50g)	24.5	At start of boil
Challenger 7.0%	1¼oz (33g)	0.0	At end of boil

Other			
Irish moss	1 tsp		For last 15 mins of boil

TO FERMENT

FERMENTATION 68°F (20°C)   **CONDITIONING** 6 weeks at 54°F (12°C)

Yeast
Wyeast 1084 Irish Ale

A particularly light-bodied, traditional Scottish session beer, Scottish 60 Shilling is malty and dry with a crisp, clean finish.

SCOTTISH 60 SHILLING

ORIGINAL GRAVITY 1035 **EXPECTED FINAL GRAVITY** 1010 **TOTAL LIQUOR** 7.9 GALLONS (30.5 LITERS)

MAKES	READY TO DRINK	ESTIMATED ABV	BITTERNESS RATING	COLOR RATING
6 GALLONS (23 LITERS)	7 WEEKS	3.3%	11.7 IBU	18 EBC

FOR THE MASH

LIQUOR 2.2 gallons (8.6 liters)   **MASH TIME** 1 hr   **TEMPERATURE** 160°F (70°C)

Grain bill	Quantity
Pale malt	6lb 10oz (3kg)
Munich malt	6oz (175g)
Medium crystal malt	4½oz (130g)
Melanoidin malt	3½oz (100g)
Chocolate malt	1¾oz (50g)

FOR THE BOIL

LIQUOR 7 gallons (27 liters)   **BOIL TIME** 1 hr 10 mins

Hops	Quantity	IBU	When to add
Fuggle 4.5%	¾oz (21g)	11.6	At start of boil
Other			
Irish moss	1 tsp		For last 15 mins of boil

TO FERMENT

FERMENTATION 64°F (18°C)   **CONDITIONING** 6 weeks at 54°F (12°C)

Yeast
Wyeast 1728 Scottish Ale

Like many other Scottish beers, Scottish 80 Shilling
is very malty, with no hop aroma, but has a clean, neutral
finish. This is an "export" strength Scottish classic.

SCOTTISH 80 SHILLING

ORIGINAL GRAVITY 1052 EXPECTED FINAL GRAVITY 1015 TOTAL LIQUOR 8.4 GALLONS (32.5 LITERS)

MAKES 6 GALLONS (23 LITERS)	READY TO DRINK 7 WEEKS	ESTIMATED ABV 4.9%	BITTERNESS RATING 16.5 IBU	COLOR RATING 29.2 EBC

FOR THE MASH

LIQUOR 3.4 gallons (13 liters)   **MASH TIME** 1 hr   **TEMPERATURE** 160°F (70°C)

Grain bill	Quantity
Pale malt	10lb 2oz (4.6kg)
Caramunich II malt	10½oz (300g)
Medium crystal malt	7oz (200g)
Carafa III malt	2¾oz (80g)

FOR THE BOIL

LIQUOR 7 gallons (27 liters)   **BOIL TIME** 1 hr 10 mins

Hops	Quantity	IBU	When to add
Golding 5.5%	1oz (27g)	16.5	At start of boil
Other			
Irish moss	1 tsp		For last 15 mins of boil

TO FERMENT

FERMENTATION 64°F (18°C)   **CONDITIONING** 6 weeks at 54°F (12°C)

Yeast
Wyeast 1728 Scottish Ale

MALT EXTRACT VERSION

Steep 10½oz (300g) **Caramunich II malt**, 7oz (200g)
medium crystal malt, and 2¾oz (80g) **Carafa III malt** in
7 gallons (27 liters) water at 149°F (65°C) for 30 mins.
Remove the malt, then add 6lb 6oz (2.9kg) **dried light
malt extract**, bring to a boil, and add the hops as
specified in the main recipe.

An artisan farmhouse ale from northern France, this "beer for keeping" was traditionally brewed in early spring and lagered until the summer. It has a lovely, malty sweetness.

BIÈRE DE GARDE

ORIGINAL GRAVITY 1065 **EXPECTED FINAL GRAVITY** 1014 **TOTAL LIQUOR** 8.3 GALLONS (32 LITERS)

MAKES	READY TO DRINK	ESTIMATED ABV	BITTERNESS RATING	COLOR RATING
6 GALLONS (23 LITERS)	7 WEEKS	7%	25 IBU	17.7 EBC

FOR THE MASH

LIQUOR 4.8 gallons (18.4 liters) **MASH TIME** 1 hr **TEMPERATURE** 149°F (65°C)

Grain bill	Quantity
Pale malt	8lb 13oz (4kg)
Vienna malt	3lb 3oz (1.5kg)
Aromatic malt	1lb 2oz (500g)
Biscuit malt	1lb 2oz (500g)

FOR THE BOIL

LIQUOR 7 gallons (27 liters) **BOIL TIME** 1 hr 10 mins

Hops	Quantity	IBU	When to add
Brewers Gold 7%	1¼oz (33g)	22.9	At start of boil
Tettnang 4.5%	1oz (25g)	2.1	For last 5 mins of boil
Tettnang 4.5%	1oz (25g)	0.0	At end of boil
Other			
Irish moss	1 tsp		For last 15 mins of boil

TO FERMENT

FERMENTATION 72°F (22°C) **CONDITIONING** 6 weeks at 54°F (12°C)

Yeast
Wyeast 3711 French Saison

Traditionally brewed in the fall to take advantage of the bounty of malts from the grain harvest, spices can be added to this delicious winter beer for a festive treat.

WINTER WARMER

ORIGINAL GRAVITY 1062 **EXPECTED FINAL GRAVITY** 1015 **TOTAL LIQUOR** 8.5 GALLONS (32.5 LITERS)

MAKES	READY TO DRINK	ESTIMATED ABV	BITTERNESS RATING	COLOR RATING
6 GALLONS (23 LITERS)	8 WEEKS	6.2%	19.6 IBU	27.2 EBC

FOR THE MASH

LIQUOR 3.6 gallons (13.75 liters) **MASH TIME** 1 hr **TEMPERATURE** 149°F (65°C)

Grain bill	Quantity	Grain bill	Quantity
Pale malt	11lb 4oz (5.1kg)	Torrified wheat malt	3½oz (100g)
Medium crystal malt	7oz (200g)	Chocolate malt	3½oz (100g)

FOR THE BOIL

LIQUOR 7 gallons (27 liters) **BOIL TIME** 1 hr 10 mins

Hops	Quantity	IBU	When to add
East Kent Golding 5.5%	1oz (30g)	17.5	At start of boil
Progress 5.5%	⅓oz (10g)	2.1	For last 10 mins of boil
Target 10.5%	⅓oz (10g)	0.0	At end of boil

Other			
Irish moss	1 tsp		For last 15 mins of boil
Honey	1lb 2oz (500g)		For last 5 mins of boil

TO FERMENT

FERMENTATION 68°F (20°C) **CONDITIONING** 6 weeks at 54°F (12°C)

Yeast
Wyeast 1968 London ESB Ale

MALT EXTRACT VERSION

Steep 7oz (200g) **medium crystal malt** and 3½oz (100g) **chocolate malt** in 7 gallons (27 liters) water at 149°F (65°C) for 30 mins. Remove the malt, then add 7lb 4oz (3.3kg) **light dried malt extract**, bring to a boil, and add the hops as specified in the main recipe.

BREWER'S TIP

After 4 days, steep 1 tsp cinnamon and 1 tbsp grated ginger in 2fl oz (50ml) vodka for 15 mins, then add this mixture to the fermenter for 1 week before bottling.

A dark and malty festive brew with a subtle hint of Christmas spices, this strong, special beer should be left to mature for three months before being savored.

CHRISTMAS ALE

ORIGINAL GRAVITY 1063 **EXPECTED FINAL GRAVITY** 1012 **TOTAL LIQUOR** 8.5 GALLONS (32.5 LITERS)

MAKES 6 GALLONS (23 LITERS)	READY TO DRINK 12 WEEKS	ESTIMATED ABV 6.8%	BITTERNESS RATING 25 IBU	COLOR RATING 30.7 EBC

FOR THE MASH

LIQUOR 3.6 gallons (14 liters)   **MASH TIME** 1 hr   **TEMPERATURE** 149°F (67°C)

Grain bill	Quantity
Pale malt	9lb 11oz (4.4kg)
Biscuit malt	1lb 2oz (500g)
Caramunich I	12oz (350g)
Medium crystal malt	10½oz (300g)
Torrified wheat malt	3½oz (100g)
Carafa special I malt	3½oz (100g)

FOR THE BOIL

LIQUOR 7 gallons (27 liters)   **BOIL TIME** 1 hr 10 mins

Hops	Quantity	IBU	When to add
Challenger 7%	⅔oz (18g)	13.2	At start of boil
Styrian Golding 4.5%	1oz (26g)	5.9	For last 15 mins of boil
Styrian Golding 4.5%	1oz (26g)	0.0	At end of boil

Other			
Irish moss	1 tsp		For last 15 mins of boil
Star anise	⅓oz (10g)		For last 10 mins of boil
Cinnamon sticks	2 sticks		For last 10 mins of boil
Ground nutmeg	1 tsp		For last 10 mins of boil
Light candi crystals	1lb 2oz (500g)		For last 5 mins of boil

TO FERMENT

FERMENTATION 72°F (22°C)   **CONDITIONING** 8 weeks at 54°F (12°C)

Yeast
Wyeast 1028 London Ale

Traditionally, each Belgian monastery created its own
unique style of high-quality beer. This example has
a complex malty flavor with spicy alcohol notes.

ABBEY BEER

ORIGINAL GRAVITY 1060 EXPECTED FINAL GRAVITY 1013 TOTAL LIQUOR 8.6 GALLONS (33 LITERS)

MAKES	READY TO	ESTIMATED	BITTERNESS	COLOR
6 GALLONS	DRINK	ABV	RATING	RATING
(23 LITERS)	7 WEEKS	6.4%	19.8 IBU	12.1 EBC

FOR THE MASH

LIQUOR 3.9 gallons (15 liters) MASH TIME 1 hr TEMPERATURE 149°F (65°C)

Grain bill	Quantity
Belgian Pilsner malt	10lb (4.5kg)
Vienna malt	2¼lb (1kg)
Biscuit malt	1lb 2oz (500g)

FOR THE BOIL

LIQUOR 7 gallons (27 liters) BOIL TIME 1 hr 15 mins

Hops	Quantity	IBU	When to add
Perle 8%	¾oz (21g)	17.5	At start of boil
Styrian Golding 5.5%	¾oz (21g)	2.3	For last 5 mins of boil

Other			
Irish moss	1 tsp		For last 15 mins of boil

TO FERMENT

FERMENTATION 72°F (22°C) CONDITIONING 6 weeks at 54°F (12°C)

Yeast
Wyeast 1214 Belgian Abbey Style Ale

153

A strong, straw-colored ale originating from Belgium, the malty sweetness in this brew is complemented by a spicy, slightly hoppy aroma and a dry, candi-sugar finish.

BELGIAN BLONDE ALE

ORIGINAL GRAVITY 1070 EXPECTED FINAL GRAVITY 1015 TOTAL LIQUOR 8.7 GALLONS (33.5 LITERS)

MAKES	READY TO DRINK	ESTIMATED ABV	BITTERNESS RATING	COLOR RATING
6 GALLONS (23 LITERS)	8 WEEKS	7.4%	18 IBU	12.9 EBC

FOR THE MASH

LIQUOR 4.2 gallons (16.25 liters)   **MASH TIME** 1 hr   **TEMPERATURE** 149°F (65°C)

Grain bill	Quantity
Pilsner malt	13lb 4oz (6kg)
Caravienne malt	9oz (250g)
Caramunich I malt	9oz (250g)

FOR THE BOIL

LIQUOR 7 gallons (27 liters)   **BOIL TIME** 1 hr 10 mins

Hops	Quantity	IBU	When to add
East Kent Golding 5.5%	1oz (30g)	16.1	At start of boil
Styrian Golding 5.5%	⅓oz (10g)	1.9	For last 10 mins of boil
Styrian Golding 5.5%	⅔oz (20g)	0.0	At end of boil

Other			
Irish moss	1 tsp		For last 15 mins of boil
Belgian candi sugar light	10½oz (300g)		For last 5 mins of boil

TO FERMENT

FERMENTATION 72°F (22°C)   **CONDITIONING** 6 weeks at 54°F (12°C)

Yeast
Wyeast 1388 Belgian Strong Ale

MALT EXTRACT VERSION

Steep 9oz (250g) **Caravienne malt** and 9oz (250g) **Caramunich I malt** in 7 gallons (27 liters) water at 149°F (65°C) for 30 mins. Remove the malt, then add 8lb 6oz (3.8kg) **dried extra-light malt extract**, bring to a boil, and add the hops as specified in the main recipe.

A complex, malty sweetness combined with moderate fruitiness make this Belgian classic a real delight. It is strong, deep red in color, and has a lovely, spicy flavor.

BELGIAN DUBBEL

ORIGINAL GRAVITY 1066 **EXPECTED FINAL GRAVITY** 1014 **TOTAL LIQUOR** 8.6 GALLONS (33 LITERS)

MAKES 6 GALLONS (23 LITERS)	READY TO DRINK 8 WEEKS	ESTIMATED ABV 6.9%	BITTERNESS RATING 20.5 IBU	COLOR RATING 29.2 EBC

FOR THE MASH

LIQUOR 3.9 gallons (15 liters) **MASH TIME** 1 hr **TEMPERATURE** 149°F (65°C)

Grain bill	Quantity
Belgian Pilsner malt	11lb 11oz (5.3kg)
Special B malt	14oz (400g)
Caramunich I malt	10½oz (300g)

FOR THE BOIL

LIQUOR 7 gallons (27 liters) **BOIL TIME** 1 hr 10 mins

Hops	Quantity	IBU	When to add
Hallertauer Hersbrucker 3.5%	1¼oz (35g)	12.7	At start of boil
Tettnang 4.5%	1¼oz (35g)	7.5	For last 15 mins of boil

Other			
Irish moss	1 tsp		For last 15 mins of boil
Belgian light candi crystals	14oz (400g)		For last 5 mins of boil

TO FERMENT

FERMENTATION 72°F (22°C) **CONDITIONING** 7 weeks at 54°F (12°C)

Yeast
Wyeast 3944 Belgian Witbier

MALT EXTRACT VERSION

Steep 14oz (400g) **Special B malt** and 10½oz (300g) **Caramunich I malt** in 7 gallons (27 liters) water at 149°F (65°C) for 30 mins. Remove the malt, then add 7½lb (3.4kg) **dried extra-light malt extract**, bring to a boil, and add the hops and other ingredients as specified in the main recipe.

With less complex malt flavors than its cousin Dubbel
(see opposite), Belgian Tripel has a crisp, tart finish.
Although high in alcohol, it doesn't taste overpowering.

BELGIAN TRIPEL

ORIGINAL GRAVITY 1080 EXPECTED FINAL GRAVITY 1013 TOTAL LIQUOR 8.7 GALLONS (33.5 LITERS)

MAKES	READY TO DRINK	ESTIMATED ABV	BITTERNESS RATING	COLOR RATING
6 GALLONS (23 LITERS)	12 WEEKS	9.1%	30.2 IBU	11.4 EBC

FOR THE MASH

LIQUOR 4.2 gallons (16.3 liters) MASH TIME 1 hr TEMPERATURE 149°F (65°C)

Grain bill	Quantity
Belgian Pilsner malt	14lb (6.3kg)
Caramunich I malt	9oz (250g)

FOR THE BOIL

LIQUOR 7 gallons (27 liters) BOIL TIME 1 hr 10 mins

Hops	Quantity	IBU	When to add
Saaz 4.2%	1¾oz (50g)	18.6	At start of boil
Styrian Golding 5.5%	1¾oz (50g)	11.7	For last 15 mins of boil

Other			
Irish moss	1 tsp		Fot last 15 mins of boil
Belgian light candi crystals	2¼lb (1kg)		For last 5 mins of boil

TO FERMENT

FERMENTATION 75°F (24°C) CONDITIONING 11 weeks at 54°F (12°C))

Yeast
Wyeast 1388 Belgian Strong Ale

MALT EXTRACT VERSION

Steep 9oz (250g) **Caramunich I malt** in 7 gallons (27 liters)
water at 149°F (65°C) for 30 mins. Remove the malt, then
add 8lb 13oz (4kg) **dried extra-light malt extract**, bring to
a boil, and add the hops and other ingredients as specified
in the main recipe.

Created by the Moortgat Brewery in Belgium at the end
of World War I, this style is similar to Tripel (see p157)
but paler, less malty, and with a slightly bitter finish.

BELGIAN STRONG GOLDEN ALE

ORIGINAL GRAVITY 1072 **EXPECTED FINAL GRAVITY** 1012 **TOTAL LIQUOR** 8.6 GALLONS (33 LITERS)

MAKES	READY TO	ESTIMATED	BITTERNESS	COLOR
6 GALLONS	DRINK	ABV	RATING	RATING
(23 LITERS)	8 WEEKS	7.9%	30 IBU	10 EBC

FOR THE MASH

LIQUOR 3.9 gallons (15 liters)   **MASH TIME** 1 hr   **TEMPERATURE** 149°F (65°C)

Grain bill	Quantity
Belgian Pilsner malt	12lb 6oz (5.6kg)
Carapils malt	1lb (450g)
Aromatic malt	10½oz (300g)

FOR THE BOIL

LIQUOR 7 gallons (27 liters)   **BOIL TIME** 1 hr 10 mins

Hops	Quantity	IBU	When to add
Saaz 4.2%	1⅔oz (47g)	18.6	At start of boil
Tettnang 4.5%	2oz (58g)	11.7	For last 15 mins of boil

Other			
Irish moss	1 tsp		For last 15 mins of boil
Belgian light candi crystals	1lb 10oz (750g)		For last 5 mins of boil

TO FERMENT

FERMENTATION 75°F (24°C)   **CONDITIONING** 7 weeks at 54°F (12°C)

Yeast
Wyeast Belgian Abbey Style Ale II

MALT EXTRACT VERSION

Steep 1lb (450g) **Carapils malt** in 7 gallons (27 liters)
water at 149°F (65°C) for 30 mins. Remove the malt, then
add 8lb (3.6kg) **dried extra-light malt extract**, bring to a
boil, and add the hops as specified in the main recipe.

An easy version of a barrel-aged beer, this ale is dark brown and full of complex malt character, combined with oak and vanilla flavors. It's one to let age.

OAKED BROWN ALE

ORIGINAL GRAVITY 1089 **EXPECTED FINAL GRAVITY** 1019 **TOTAL LIQUOR** 75 PINTS (43 LITERS)

MAKES	READY TO DRINK	ESTIMATED ABV	BITTERNESS RATING	COLOR RATING
6 GALLONS (23 LITERS)	9 WEEKS	9.4%	60.5 IBU	47.2 EBC

FOR THE MASH

LIQUOR 6.3 gallons (24 liters)   **MASH TIME** 1 hr   **TEMPERATURE** 151°F (66°C)

Grain bill	Quantity	Grain bill	Quantity
Pale malt	15lb (7.4kg)	Light crystal malt	7oz (200g)
Rye malt	1lb 10oz (750g)	German Carafa I	3½oz (100g)
Flaked oats	1lb 5oz (600g)	Roasted barley	3½oz (100g)
Brown malt	1lb 2oz (500g)	Dark crystal malt	2¾oz (80g)

FOR THE BOIL

LIQUOR 7 gallons (27 liters)   **BOIL TIME** 1 hr 15 mins

Hops	Quantity	IBU	When to add
Magnum 11%	1¾oz (50g)	60.5	At start of boil

Other			
Irish moss	1 tsp		For last 15 mins of boil

TO FERMENT

FERMENTATION 68°F (20°C)   **CONDITIONING** 6 weeks at 50°F (10°C)

Yeast
White Labs WLP001 California Ale

Other	Quantity	When to add
American light oak chips	1¾oz (50g)	After fermentation is complete, leave for 2 weeks

BREWER'S TIP

Rack the beer into a clean vessel before adding the chips. Remove once the desired level of oaky flavor is achieved.

Stronger, paler, and less sweet than its southern counterpart, Northern Brown Ale has a nutty, chocolaty character with a moderately hoppy finish.

NORTHERN BROWN ALE

ORIGINAL GRAVITY 1052 **EXPECTED FINAL GRAVITY** 1013 **TOTAL LIQUOR** 8.4 GALLONS (32.5 LITERS)

MAKES	READY TO DRINK	ESTIMATED ABV	BITTERNESS RATING	COLOR RATING
6 GALLONS (23 LITERS)	6 WEEKS	5.1 %	25.7 IBU	27.2 EBC

FOR THE MASH

LIQUOR 3.4 gallons (13 liters)   **MASH TIME** 1 hr   **TEMPERATURE** 149°F (65°C)

Grain bill	Quantity
Pale malt	10lb 9oz (4.8kg)
Medium crystal malt	9oz (250g)
Chocolate malt	3½oz (100g)

FOR THE BOIL

LIQUOR 7 gallons (27 liters)   **BOIL TIME** 1 hr 10 mins

Hops	Quantity	IBU	When to add
Admiral 14.5%	½oz (16g)	25.7	At start of boil
Challenger 7.0%	½oz (16g)	0.0	At end of boil

Other			
Irish moss	1 tsp		For last 15 mins of boil

TO FERMENT

FERMENTATION 68°F (20°C)   **CONDITIONING** 5 weeks at 54°F (12°C)

Yeast
Wyeast 1098 British Ale

MALT EXTRACT VERSION
Steep 9oz (250g) **medium crystal malt** and 3½oz (100g) **chocolate malt** in 7 gallons (27 liters) water at 149°F (65°C) for 30 mins. Remove the malt, then add 7lb 4oz (3.3kg) **dried light malt extract**, bring to a boil, and add the hops as specified in the main recipe.

Also known as London ale, this style originated in the early 20th century as an alternative to porter and mild. Moderately low in alcohol, it has a sweet, malty finish.

SOUTHERN BROWN ALE

ORIGINAL GRAVITY 1041 **EXPECTED FINAL GRAVITY** 1012 **TOTAL LIQUOR** 8.1 GALLONS (31 LITERS)

MAKES 6 GALLONS (23 LITERS)	READY TO DRINK 4 WEEKS	ESTIMATED ABV 3.8%	BITTERNESS RATING 17.4 IBU	COLOR RATING 37.6 EBC

FOR THE MASH

LIQUOR 2.6 gallons (10 liters)   **MASH TIME** 1 hr   **TEMPERATURE** 149°F (65°C)

Grain bill	Quantity		Grain bill	Quantity
Pale malt	7lb 11oz (3.5kg)		Torrified wheat	3½oz (100g)
Dark crystal malt	10½oz (300g)		Black malt	2oz (55g)
Chocolate malt	4oz (110g)			

FOR THE BOIL

LIQUOR 7 gallons (27 liters)   **BOIL TIME** 1 hr 10 mins

Hops	Quantity	IBU	When to add
Fuggle 4.5%	¾oz (24g)	12.9	At start of boil
Fuggle 4.5%	¾oz (24g)	4.5	For last 10 mins of boil
Other			
Irish moss	1 tsp		For last 15 mins of boil

TO FERMENT

FERMENTATION 72°F (22°C)   **CONDITIONING** 3 weeks at 54°F (12°C)

Yeast
Wyeast 1187 Ringwood Ale

MALT EXTRACT VERSION
Steep 10½oz (300g) **dark crystal malt**, 4oz (110g) **chocolate malt**, and 2oz (55g) **black malt** in 7 gallons (27 liters) water at 149°F (65°C) for 30 mins. Remove the malt, then add 5lb 1oz (2.3kg) **dried light malt extract**, bring to a boil, and add the hops as specified in the main recipe.

BREWER'S TIP

If you would prefer a slightly drier-tasting beer, try using Wyeast 1099 Whitbread Ale instead of the Ringwood.

Dark and strong with fruity, sherrylike flavors
from the corn sugar, this special beer requires a long
conditioning period to fully develop its character.

OLD ALE

ORIGINAL GRAVITY 1079 **EXPECTED FINAL GRAVITY** 1014 **TOTAL LIQUOR** 8.8 GALLONS (34 LITERS)

MAKES 6 GALLONS (23 LITERS)	READY TO DRINK 12 WEEKS	ESTIMATED ABV 8.7%	BITTERNESS RATING 55 IBU	COLOR RATING 32.6 EBC

FOR THE MASH

LIQUOR 4.4 gallons (16.75 liters)   **MASH TIME** 1 hr   **TEMPERATURE** 154°F (68°C)

Grain bill	Quantity
Pale malt	10lb (4.5kg)
Munich malt	4lb (1.8kg)
Dark crystal malt	10½oz (300g)
Chocolate malt	3½oz (100g)

FOR THE BOIL

LIQUOR 7 gallons (27 liters)   **BOIL TIME** 1 hr 10 mins

Hops	Quantity	IBU	When to add
Golding 5.5%	2¾oz (76g)	37.3	At start of boil
Golding 5.5%	2¾oz (76g)	13.1	For last 10 mins of boil

Other			
Irish moss	1 tsp		For last 15 mins of boil
Corn sugar	1lb 7oz (650g)		For last 5 mins of boil

TO FERMENT

FERMENTATION 68°F (20°C)   **CONDITIONING** 11 weeks at 54°F (12°C)

Yeast
Wyeast 1028 London Ale

BREWER'S TIP

To give your beer a festive
twist, try adding some
Christmas spices to the
fermenter. Cinnamon, nutmeg,
and cloves will all work well.

A traditional British-style Mild, this dark ale is
moderately low in alcohol with fruity, chocolaty,
malt flavors and a dry, hoppy finish.

MILD

ORIGINAL GRAVITY 1036 **EXPECTED FINAL GRAVITY** 1011 **TOTAL LIQUOR** 7.8 GALLONS (30 LITERS)

MAKES	READY TO DRINK	ESTIMATED ABV	BITTERNESS RATING	COLOR RATING
6 GALLONS (23 LITERS)	4 WEEKS	3.3 %	21.2 IBU	33.5 EBC

FOR THE MASH

LIQUOR 2.3 gallons (9 liters)   **MASH TIME** 1 hr   **TEMPERATURE** 154°F (68°C)

Grain bill	Quantity
Pale malt	6lb 10oz (3kg)
Dark crystal malt	1lb 2oz (500g)
Chocolate malt	3½oz (100g)

FOR THE BOIL

LIQUOR 7 gallons (27 liters)   **BOIL TIME** 1 hr 10 mins

Hops	Quantity	IBU	When to add
Northdown 8%	⅔oz (20g)	19.7	At start of boil
Bramling Cross 6.0%	⅓oz (10g)	0.0	For last 5 mins of boil

Other			
Irish moss	1 tsp		For last 15 mins of boil

TO FERMENT

FERMENTATION 68°F (20°C)   **CONDITIONING** 3 weeks at 54°F (12°C)

Yeast
Wyeast 1318 London Ale III

MALT EXTRACT VERSION

Steep 1lb 2oz (500g) **dark crystal malt** and 3½oz (100g)
chocolate malt in 7 gallons (27 liters) water at 149°F
(65°C) for 30 mins. Remove the malt, then add 4lb 3oz
(1.9kg) **dried light malt extract**, bring to a boil, and add
the hops as specified in the main recipe.

This dark, strong ale has delicious malty and chocolaty flavors balanced by a light, hoppy bitterness. Ruby Mild is perfect served with a steak and fries.

RUBY MILD

ORIGINAL GRAVITY 1049   **EXPECTED FINAL GRAVITY** 1014   **TOTAL LIQUOR** 8.3 GALLONS (32 LITERS)

MAKES	READY TO DRINK	ESTIMATED ABV	BITTERNESS RATING	COLOR RATING
6 GALLONS (23 LITERS)	8 WEEKS	4.6%	18.1 IBU	31.6 EBC

FOR THE MASH

LIQUOR 3.2 gallons (12.3 liters)   **MASH TIME** 1 hr   **TEMPERATURE** 150°F (66°C)

Grain bill	Quantity
Pale malt	10lb (4.5kg)
Medium crystal malt	5½oz (150g)
Chocolate malt	5½oz (150g)
Torrified wheat malt	4½oz (125g)

FOR THE BOIL

LIQUOR 7 gallons (27 liters)   **BOIL TIME** 1 hr 10 mins

Hops	Quantity	IBU	When to add
Golding 5.5%	1oz (30g)	18.1	At start of boil
Golding 5.5%	½oz (15g)	0.0	At end of boil

Other			
Irish moss	1 tsp		For last 15 mins of boil

TO FERMENT

FERMENTATION 72°F (22°C)   **CONDITIONING** at least 4 weeks at 54°F (12°C)

Yeast
Wyeast 1187 Ringwood Ale

MALT EXTRACT VERSION
Steep 5½oz (150g) **medium crystal malt** and 5½oz (150g) **chocolate malt** in 7 gallons (27 liters) water at 149°F (65°C) for 30 mins. Remove the malt, then add 6lb 6oz (2.9kg) **dried light malt extract**, bring to a boil, and add the hops as specified in the main recipe.

One of the strongest beers brewed by any brewery, English Barley Wine has a complex, malty, sherrylike flavor with a lingering hoppy bitterness on the finish.

ENGLISH BARLEY WINE

ORIGINAL GRAVITY 1090 **EXPECTED FINAL GRAVITY** 1019 **TOTAL LIQUOR** 9.1 GALLONS (35.5 LITERS)

MAKES	READY TO DRINK	ESTIMATED ABV	BITTERNESS RATING	COLOR RATING
6 GALLONS (23 LITERS)	15 WEEKS	9.6%	50 IBU	27.3 EBC

FOR THE MASH

LIQUOR 5.5 gallons (21 liters)   **MASH TIME** 1 hr   **TEMPERATURE** 153°F (67°C)

Grain bill	Quantity
Pale malt	16lb (7.2kg)
Dark crystal malt	10½oz (300g)
Carapils malt	1¾lb (800g)

FOR THE BOIL

LIQUOR 7 gallons (27 liters)   **BOIL TIME** 1 hr 30 mins

Hops	Quantity	IBU	When to add
Northdown 8.0%	2½oz (71g)	50.0	At start of boil
East Kent Golding 5.5%	½oz (14g)	0.0	At end of boil
Target 10.5%	½oz (14g)	0.0	At end of boil

Other			
Irish moss	1 tsp		For last 15 mins of boil
Honey	1lb 2oz (500g)		For last 5 mins of boil

TO FERMENT

FERMENTATION 72°F (22°C)   **CONDITIONING** 14 weeks at 54°F (12°C)

Yeast
Wyeast 1028 London Ale

MALT EXTRACT VERSION

Steep 10½oz (300g) **dark crystal malt** and 1¾lb (800g) **Carapils malt** in 7 gallons (27 liters) water at 149°F (65°C) for 30 mins. Remove the malt, then add 10lb (4.5kg) **dried light malt extract**, bring to a boil, and add the hops as specified in the main recipe.

BREWER'S TIP

If your mash tun isn't large enough for all the malts in the grain bill, reduce the pale malt to 11lb (5kg) and add 2lb 14oz (1.3kg) dried malt extract to the boil.

Far hoppier than its English counterpart, American
Barley Wine is a strong and intense style of beer with
a bittersweet aftertaste and robust citrus aroma.

AMERICAN BARLEY WINE

ORIGINAL GRAVITY 1105 **EXPECTED FINAL GRAVITY** 1024 **TOTAL LIQUOR** 9.8 GALLONS (37.5 LITERS)

MAKES	READY TO	ESTIMATED	BITTERNESS	COLOR
6 GALLONS	DRINK	ABV	RATING	RATING
(23 LITERS)	15 WEEKS	10.9%	66 IBU	25.4 EBC

FOR THE MASH

LIQUOR 6.8 gallons (26 liters)   **MASH TIME** 1 hr   **TEMPERATURE** 153°F (67°C)

Grain bill	Quantity
Pale malt	22lb 1oz (10kg)
Medium crystal malt	14oz (400g)
Carafa special III malt	1oz (30g)

FOR THE BOIL

LIQUOR 7 gallons (27 liters)   **BOIL TIME** 1 hr 10 mins

Hops	Quantity	IBU	When to add
Chinook 13.3%	2½oz (71g)	61.7	At start of boil
Cascade 6.6%	1oz (26g)	4.3	For last 10 mins of boil
Cascade 6.6%	3½oz (100g)	0.0	At end of boil

Other			
Irish moss	1 tsp		For last 15 mins of boil

TO FERMENT

FERMENTATION 4 days at 64°F (18°C), then 72°F (22°C) until completion
CONDITIONING 13 weeks at 54°F (12°C)

Yeast
Wyeast 1056 American Ale

MALT EXTRACT VERSION

Steep 14oz (400g) **medium crystal malt** and 1oz (30g)
Carafa special III malt in 7 gallons (27 liters) water at
149°F (65°C) for 30 mins. Remove the malt, then add 14lb
(6.3kg) **dried light malt extract**, bring to a boil, and add
the hops as specified in the main recipe.

BREWER'S TIP

The amount of grain needed
to brew this beer may
overwhelm your mash tun
volume. If this is the case,
consider making a half batch.

A soft, sweet beer with lovely caramel flavors, this brew
has more substance and roasted flavors than a brown
ale and has a delicious chocolate aftertaste.

BROWN PORTER

ORIGINAL GRAVITY 1049 EXPECTED FINAL GRAVITY 1012 TOTAL LIQUOR 8.3 GALLONS (32 LITERS)

MAKES 6 GALLONS (23 LITERS)	READY TO DRINK 5 WEEKS	ESTIMATED ABV 4.9%	BITTERNESS RATING 30.2 IBU	COLOR RATING 45 EBC

FOR THE MASH

LIQUOR 3.3 gallons (12.5 liters)   MASH TIME 1 hr   TEMPERATURE 153°F (67°C)

Grain bill	Quantity
Pale malt	8lb 13oz (4kg)
Dark crystal malt	12oz (350g)
Chocolate malt	7oz (200g)
Brown malt	10½oz (300g)

FOR THE BOIL

LIQUOR 7 gallons (27 liters)   BOIL TIME 1 hr 10 mins

Hops	Quantity	IBU	When to add
First Gold 8.0%	1oz (31g)	27.6	At start of boil
First Gold 8.0%	½oz (15g)	2.7	For last 10 mins of boil
Other			
Irish moss	1 tsp		For last 15 mins of boil

TO FERMENT

FERMENTATION 64°F (18°C)   CONDITIONING 4 weeks at 54°F (12°C)

Yeast
Wyeast 1028 London Ale

MALT EXTRACT VERSION

Steep 12oz (350g) **dark crystal malt**, 7oz (200g)
chocolate malt, and 10½oz (300g) **brown malt** in 7
gallons (27 liters) water at 149°F (65°C) for 30 mins.
Remove the malt, then add 5½lb (2.5kg) **dried light malt
extract**, bring to a boil, and add the hops as specified in
the main recipe.

Rich and smoky malt flavors combine perfectly with subtle red-berry flavors to create this irresistible, dark, reddish-brown winter ale.

SMOKED PORTER

ORIGINAL GRAVITY 1054 **EXPECTED FINAL GRAVITY** 1016 **TOTAL LIQUOR** 8.6 GALLONS (33 LITERS)

MAKES 6 GALLONS (23 LITERS)	READY TO DRINK 6 WEEKS	ESTIMATED ABV 5.1%	BITTERNESS RATING 28 IBU	COLOR RATING 49.6 EBC

FOR THE MASH

LIQUOR 3.8 gallons (14.75 liters) **MASH TIME** 1 hr **TEMPERATURE** 149°F (65°C)

Grain bill	Quantity
Pale malt	10lb (4.5kg)
Smoked malt	1lb 8oz (700g)
Black malt	10½oz (300g)
Medium crystal malt	7oz (200g)
Caramunich I malt	7oz (200g)

FOR THE BOIL

LIQUOR 7 gallons (27 liters) **BOIL TIME** 1 hr 15 mins

Hops	Quantity	IBU	When to add
Challenger 7.0%	1¼oz (35g)	23.8	At start of boil
Willamette 6.3%	⅔oz (20g)	4.2	For last 10 mins of boil
Willamette 6.3%	⅔oz (20g)	0.0	At end of boil
Other			
Irish moss	1 tsp		For last 15 mins of boil

TO FERMENT

FERMENTATION 64°F (18°C) **CONDITIONING** 5 weeks at 54°F (12°C)

Yeast
Wyeast 1187 Ringwood Ale

BREWER'S TIP

For heightened smokiness, try adding 3½oz (100g) toasted oak chips to the fermenter after 4 days.

A strong, warming beer with complex fruit flavors and a smooth, clean finish. As the name suggests, this porter originates from countries bordering the Baltic Sea.

BALTIC PORTER

ORIGINAL GRAVITY 1080   EXPECTED FINAL GRAVITY 1019   TOTAL LIQUOR 9.1 GALLONS (35 LITERS)

MAKES 6 GALLONS (23 LITERS)	READY TO DRINK 12+ WEEKS	ESTIMATED ABV 8.2%	BITTERNESS RATING 30.2 IBU	COLOR RATING 56.3 EBC

FOR THE MASH

LIQUOR 5 gallons (19.2 liters)   **MASH TIME** 1 hr   **TEMPERATURE** 153°F (67°C)

Grain bill	Quantity
Munich malt	15lb 5oz (7kg)
Amber malt	10½oz (300g)
Carafa special III	10oz (286g)
Biscuit malt	7oz (200g)
Chocolate malt	10½oz (300g)
Caramunich I	3½oz (100g)

FOR THE BOIL

LIQUOR 7 gallons (27 liters)   **BOIL TIME** 1 hr 10 mins

Hops	Quantity	IBU	When to add
Saaz 4.2%	2½oz (74g)	27.4	At start of boil
Saaz 4.2%	½oz (15g)	2.6	For last 15 mins of boil
Other			
Irish moss	1 tsp		For last 15 mins of boil

TO FERMENT

FERMENTATION 54°F (12°C)   **CONDITIONING** 11+ weeks at 54°F (12°C)

Yeast
Wyeast 2633 Oktoberfest Lager Blend

BREWER'S TIP

This beer will continue to age extremely well, so bottle it and leave for as long as possible for a superior quality brew.

This is a dark, complex, and full-bodied ale with a dry finish. It is similar in style to Brown Porter (see p169) but has a unique character thanks to the addition of honey.

HONEY PORTER

ORIGINAL GRAVITY 1048 **EXPECTED FINAL GRAVITY** 1009 **TOTAL LIQUOR** 8.3 GALLONS (32 LITERS)

MAKES 6 GALLONS (23 LITERS)	READY TO DRINK 6 WEEKS	ESTIMATED ABV 5.2%	BITTERNESS RATING 19.8 IBU	COLOR RATING 50.3 EBC

FOR THE MASH

LIQUOR 2.7 gallons (10.5 liters) **MASH TIME** 1 hr **TEMPERATURE** 149°F (65°C)

Grain bill	Quantity
Pale malt	6lb 10oz (3kg)
Light crystal malt	1lb 2oz (500g)
Vienna malt	14oz (400g)
Carafa special III	7oz (200g)
Chocolate malt	3½oz (100g)

FOR THE BOIL

LIQUOR 7 gallons (27 liters) **BOIL TIME** 1 hr 10 mins

Hops	Quantity	IBU	When to add
Fuggle 4.5%	¾oz (23g)	10.8	At start of boil
Challenger 7.0%	½oz (15g)	4.3	For last 10 mins of boil
Wakatu 6.6%	½oz (16g)	0.0	At end of boil
Other			
Irish moss	1 tsp		For last 15 mins of boil
Honey	1lb 2oz (500g)		For last 5 mins of boil

TO FERMENT

FERMENTATION 64°F (18°C) **CONDITIONING** 5 weeks at 54°F (12°C)

Yeast
Wyeast 1272 American Ale II

This Irish stout was first created to emulate the success of London-style porters. Creamier and more full-bodied than a porter, however, this is a classic, rich-flavored stout.

DRY STOUT

ORIGINAL GRAVITY 1048   EXPECTED FINAL GRAVITY 1013   TOTAL LIQUOR 8.3 GALLONS (32 LITERS)

MAKES	READY TO DRINK	ESTIMATED ABV	BITTERNESS RATING	COLOR RATING
6 GALLONS (23 LITERS)	5 WEEKS	4.7%	37.9 IBU	76.7 EBC

FOR THE MASH

LIQUOR 3.1 gallons (12 liters)   **MASH TIME** 1 hr   **TEMPERATURE** 153°F (67°C)

Grain bill	Quantity
Pale malt	8lb 6oz (3.8kg)
Flaked barley	1lb 2oz (500g)
Roasted barley	1lb (450g)
Chocolate malt	3½oz (100g)

FOR THE BOIL

LIQUOR 7 gallons (27 liters)   **BOIL TIME** 1 hr 10 mins

Hops	Quantity	IBU	When to add
East Kent Golding 5.5%	2oz (61g)	37.9	At start of boil
Other			
Irish moss	1 tsp		For last 15 mins of boil

TO FERMENT

FERMENTATION 64°F (18°C)   **CONDITIONING** 4 weeks at 54°F (12°C)

Yeast
Wyeast 1084 Irish Ale

With an irresistibly smooth texture and rich, roasted chocolate flavors, Oatmeal Stout is a delicious, comforting beer to be enjoyed in the winter months.

OATMEAL STOUT

ORIGINAL GRAVITY 1049 **EXPECTED FINAL GRAVITY** 1014 **TOTAL LIQUOR** 8.3 GALLONS (32 LITERS)

MAKES 6 GALLONS (23 LITERS)	READY TO DRINK 5 WEEKS	ESTIMATED ABV 4.6%	BITTERNESS RATING 30.3 IBU	COLOR RATING 43.9 EBC

FOR THE MASH

LIQUOR 3.1 gallons (12.2 liters)   **MASH TIME** 1 hr   **TEMPERATURE** 153°F (67°C)

Grain bill	Quantity
Pale malt	9lb 2oz (4.2kg)
Rolled oats	9oz (250g)
Medium crystal malt	9oz (200g)
Chocolate malt	5⅔oz (160g)
Roasted barley	2½oz (70g)

FOR THE BOIL

LIQUOR 7 gallons (27 liters)   **BOIL TIME** 1 hr 10 mins

Hops	Quantity	IBU	When to add
Challenger 7.0%	1½oz (39g)	30.3	At start of boil
Challenger 7.0%	½oz (16g)	0.0	At end of boil
Golding 5.5%	½oz (16g)	0.0	At end of boil

Other			
Irish moss	1 tsp		For last 15 mins of boil

TO FERMENT

FERMENTATION 68°F (20°C)   **CONDITIONING** 4 weeks at 54°F (12°C)

Yeast
Wyeast 1187 Ringwood Ale

BREWER'S TIP

Be careful not to introduce extra oxygen (e.g., from splashing) while bottling this beer—the addition of oats makes it susceptible to going stale.

Chocolate and rich, roasted coffee flavors complement
the light citrus hop aromas in this American-style stout.
Use freshly ground coffee for the best results.

COFFEE STOUT

ORIGINAL GRAVITY 1058 **EXPECTED FINAL GRAVITY** 1015 **TOTAL LIQUOR** 8.6 GALLONS (33 LITERS)

MAKES 6 GALLONS (23 LITERS)	READY TO DRINK 6 WEEKS	ESTIMATED ABV 5.7%	BITTERNESS RATING 40.6 IBU	COLOR RATING 79.2 EBC

FOR THE MASH

LIQUOR 3.8 gallons (14.6 liters) **MASH TIME** 1 hr **TEMPERATURE** 153°F (67°C)

Grain bill	Quantity
Pale malt	11lb (5kg)
Roasted barley malt	9oz (250g)
Carafa special I malt	9oz (250g)
Light crystal malt	7oz (200g)
Caramunich I malt	7oz (200g)
Chocolate malt	5½oz (150g)

FOR THE BOIL

LIQUOR 7 gallons (27 liters) **BOIL TIME** 1 hr 15 mins

Hops	Quantity	IBU	When to add
Magnum 16.0%	¾oz (21g)	35.5	At start of boil
Cascade 6.6%	¾oz (21g)	5.5	For last 10 mins of boil
Cascade 6.6%	¾oz (21g)	0.0	At end of boil

Other	Quantity		When to add
Irish moss	1 tsp		For last 15 mins of boil

TO FERMENT

FERMENTATION 64°F (18°C) **CONDITIONING** 5 weeks at 54°F (12°C)

Yeast
Wyeast 1084 Irish Ale

Other	Quantity	When to add
Fresh coffee	2 cups	After 4 days

Heavy citrus aromas and flavors perfectly complement the dark, bitter, roasted malt flavors in this American twist on traditional English and Irish stouts.

AMERICAN STOUT

ORIGINAL GRAVITY 1060 **EXPECTED FINAL GRAVITY** 1010 **TOTAL LIQUOR** 8.6 GALLONS (33 LITERS)

MAKES 6 GALLONS (23 LITERS)	READY TO DRINK 8 WEEKS	ESTIMATED ABV 6.2%	BITTERNESS RATING 39.9 IBU	COLOR RATING 76.7 EBC

FOR THE MASH

LIQUOR 3.9 gallons (15 liters)   **MASH TIME** 1 hr   **TEMPERATURE** 149°F (65°C)

Grain bill	Quantity
Pale malt	6lb 10oz (3kg)
Munich malt	4½lb (2kg)
Black malt	1lb 2oz (500g)
Medium crystal malt	1lb 2oz (500g)

FOR THE BOIL

LIQUOR 7 gallons (27 liters)   **BOIL TIME** 1 hr 15 mins

Hops	Quantity	IBU	When to add
Chinook 13.3%	1oz (28g)	38.1	At start of boil
Amarillo 5%	⅓oz (10g)	1.8	For last 10 mins of boil
Amarillo 5%	1¾oz (50g)	0.0	At end of boil

Other			
Irish moss	1 tsp		For last 15 mins of boil

TO FERMENT

FERMENTATION 64°F (18°C)   **CONDITIONING** 7 weeks at 54°F (12°C)

Yeast
White Labs WLP001 California Ale

Milk Stout was traditionally made by adding milk to porter—for serving to laborers at lunchtime. It is a silky smooth beer with hints of chocolate and coffee.

MILK STOUT

ORIGINAL GRAVITY 1059   **EXPECTED FINAL GRAVITY** 1018   **TOTAL LIQUOR** 8.4 GALLONS (32.5 LITERS)

MAKES 6 GALLONS (23 LITERS)	READY TO DRINK 5 WEEKS	ESTIMATED ABV 5.2%	BITTERNESS RATING 25 IBU	COLOR RATING 63.6 EBC

FOR THE MASH

LIQUOR 3.5 gallons (13.5 liters)   **MASH TIME** 1 hr   **TEMPERATURE** 153°F (67°C)

Grain bill	Quantity
Pale malt	9lb 2oz (4.2kg)
Chocolate malt	10½oz (300g)
Medium crystal malt	10½oz (300g)
Roasted barley	7oz (200g)
Flaked barley	7oz (200g)
Special B malt	7oz (200g)

FOR THE BOIL

LIQUOR 7 gallons (27 liters)   **BOIL TIME** 1 hr 15 mins

Hops	Quantity	IBU	When to add
Challenger 7.0%	1oz (29g)	21.7	At start of boil
Golding 5.5%	⅓oz (11g)	3.3	For last 15 mins of boil

Other			
Irish moss	1 tsp		For last 15 mins of boil
Lactose sugar	10½oz (300g)		For last 10 mins of boil

TO FERMENT

FERMENTATION 68°F (20°C)
CONDITIONING 4 weeks at 54°F (12°C)

Yeast
Wyeast 1318 London Ale III

BREWER'S TIP

The lactose sugar is a nonfermentable sugar, so increase the quantity if you prefer a sweeter beer.

Originally brewed in England for export to the courts
of the Russian czars, the high alcohol and hopping rates
in this beer preserved it and prevented it from freezing.

RUSSIAN IMPERIAL STOUT

ORIGINAL GRAVITY 1080 **EXPECTED FINAL GRAVITY** 1019 **TOTAL LIQUOR** 9.1 GALLONS (35 LITERS)

MAKES 6 GALLONS (23 LITERS)	**READY TO DRINK** 16 WEEKS	**ESTIMATED ABV** 8.2%	**BITTERNESS RATING** 60 IBU	**COLOR RATING** 76.3 EBC

FOR THE MASH

LIQUOR 5.2 gallons (20 liters) **MASH TIME** 1 hr **TEMPERATURE** 149°F (65°C)

Grain bill	Quantity
Pale malt	15lb 5oz (7kg)
Medium crystal malt	1lb 2oz (500g)
Roasted barley	7oz (200g)
Chocolate malt	5½oz (150g)
Carafa special III malt	5½oz (150g)

FOR THE BOIL

LIQUOR 7 gallons (27 liters) **BOIL TIME** 1 hr 15 mins

Hops	Quantity	IBU	When to add
Challenger 7.0%	2oz (61g)	37.9	At start of boil
Golding 5.5%	2oz (61g)	22.2	For last 30 mins of boil

Other			
Irish moss	1 tsp		For last 15 mins of boil

TO FERMENT

FERMENTATION 68°F (20°C) **CONDITIONING** 15 weeks at 54°F (12°C)

Yeast
Wyeast 1028 London Ale

MALT EXTRACT VERSION

Steep 1lb 2oz (500g) **medium crystal malt**, 7oz (200g) **roasted barley**,
5½oz (150g) **chocolate malt**, and 5½oz (150g) **Carafa special III malt**
in 7 gallons (27 liters) water at 149°F (65°C) for 30 mins. Remove the
malt, then add 9lb 11oz (4.4kg) **dried light malt extract**, bring to a
boil, and add the hops as specified in the main recipe.

This delicious beer combines a dark, rich maltiness, subtle vanilla aroma, and sweet bourbon finish. Brew well in advance and let mature for several months.

VANILLA BOURBON STOUT

ORIGINAL GRAVITY 1070 **EXPECTED FINAL GRAVITY** 1017 **TOTAL LIQUOR** 8.8 GALLONS (34 LITERS)

MAKES 6 GALLONS (23 LITERS)	READY TO DRINK 16 WEEKS	ESTIMATED ABV 7.8%	BITTERNESS RATING 30.2 IBU	COLOR RATING 58.6 EBC

FOR THE MASH

LIQUOR 4.6 gallons (17.5 liters)   **MASH TIME** 1 hr   **TEMPERATURE** 149°F (65°C)

Grain bill	Quantity
Pale malt	1lb 13oz (4.9kg)
Vienna malt	2½lb (1.1kg)
Brown malt	1lb 2oz (500g)
Chocolate malt	12oz (350g)
Medium crystal malt	7oz (200g)

FOR THE BOIL

LIQUOR 7 gallons (27 liters)   **BOIL TIME** 1 hr 15 mins

Hops	Quantity	IBU	When to add
Northern Brewer 8.0%	1¼oz (35g)	26.6	At start of boil
Challenger 7.0 %	½oz (16g)	3.6	For last 10 mins of boil

Other			
Irish moss	1 tsp		For last 15 mins of boil

TO FERMENT

FERMENTATION 68°F (20°C)   **CONDITIONING** 15 weeks at 54°F (12°C)

Yeast
Wyeast 1028 London Ale

Other	Quantity	When to add
Vanilla beans	2 beans	Dry hop after 4 days, leave for about 1 week
Bourbon	1¼ cups (400ml)	Just before bottling

Blueberry and coconut are a match made in heaven.
Combine this with delicious roasted malts and farmhouse yeast,
and you've got a really interesting stout.

BLUEBERRY AND COCONUT STOUT

ORIGINAL GRAVITY 1071 **EXPECTED FINAL GRAVITY** 1019 **TOTAL LIQUOR** 10.3 GALLONS (39 LITERS)

MAKES 6 GALLONS (23 LITERS)	READY TO DRINK 5 WEEKS	ESTIMATED ABV 7.1%	BITTERNESS RATING 97 IBU	COLOR RATING 74.3 EBC

FOR THE MASH

LIQUOR 5.3 gallons (20 liters) **MASH TIME** 1 hr 30 mins **TEMPERATURE** 149°F (65°C)

Grain bill	Quantity	Grain bill	Quantity
Pale malt	13lb (6.5kg)	Carafa special III	5½oz (150g)
Flaked oats	1lb 2oz (500g)	Roasted barley	5½oz (150g)
Light crystal malt	9oz (250g)	Extra dark crystal	3½oz (100g)
Chocolate malt	9oz (250g)		

FOR THE BOIL

LIQUOR 7 gallons (27 liters) **BOIL TIME** 1 hr 15 mins

Hops	Quantity	IBU	When to add
Magnum 10.2%	2¾oz (80g)	97	At start of boil

Other			
Irish moss	1 tsp		For last 15 mins of boil
Maple syrup	9fl oz (250ml)		At end of boil

TO FERMENT

FERMENTATION 68°F (20°C) **CONDITIONING** 4 weeks at 50°F (10°C)

Yeast
Omega Yeast OYL061 Voss Kveik

Other	Quantity	When to add
Flaked coconut	1lb 2oz (500g)	After fermentation
Blueberry puree	3½oz (100g), or to taste	After fermentation

BREWER'S TIP

Allow the coconut to infuse
until the desired character is
achieved. Add more if you like,
although it should be subtle.

Sweet vanilla, smooth coffee, and subtle nut characters combine with maple syrup to produce a deliciously drinkable imperial stout. Use Sumatran coffee for an extra-smooth, fruity aroma.

COFFEE, VANILLA, AND MAPLE IMPERIAL STOUT

ORIGINAL GRAVITY 1089 **EXPECTED FINAL GRAVITY** 1016 **TOTAL LIQUOR** 11.4 GALLONS (43 LITERS)

MAKES	READY TO DRINK	ESTIMATED ABV	BITTERNESS RATING	COLOR RATING
6 GALLONS (23 LITERS)	5 WEEKS	9.8%	12.6 IBU	121 EBC

FOR THE MASH

LIQUOR 6.3 gallons (24 liters) **MASH TIME** 1 hr 30 mins **TEMPERATURE** 149°F (65°C)

Grain bill	Quantity		Grain bill	Quantity
Pale malt	11lb (5.5kg)		Biscuit malt	1lb 5oz (600g)
Flaked oats	2¾lb (1.75kg)		Carafa special III	7oz (200g)
Chocolate malt	1¾lb (800g)		Roasted barley	7oz (200g)
Dark crystal	1½lb (650g)			

FOR THE BOIL

LIQUOR 7 gallons (27 liters) **BOIL TIME** 1 hr 15 mins

Hops	Quantity	IBU	When to add
Magnum 11.6%	¼oz (10g)	12.6	At start of boil

Other			
Irish moss	1 tsp		For last 15 mins of boil
Maple syrup	9fl oz (250ml)		At end of boil

TO FERMENT

FERMENTATION 68°F (20°C) **CONDITIONING** 4 weeks at 50°F (10°C)

Yeast
Wyeast 1056 American Ale

Other	Quantity	When to add
Vanilla beans	2	After fermentation
Chopped toasted almonds	10oz (300g)	After fermentation
Coffee beans, lightly crushed	3½oz (100g)	After fermentation

Leave for 48 hrs, or until desired character is achieved.

WHEAT BEERS

Widely brewed in medieval Europe, wheat beers—also known as white beers—are produced with a large ratio of wheat in the mash tun.

Wheat often makes up more than 50 percent of the grain bill in this style and is typically mixed with pale malt. This results in a hazy beer with a distinctly dry character—although most of the flavors are produced from the special strains of yeast that are used.

TOP-CROPPING YEAST

Wheat-style yeasts are true top-cropping yeasts, meaning they produce an exceptionally large krausen during fermentation since all the yeast rises to the top of the wort. The higher fermentation temperatures result in complex flavor compounds and esters being produced, which would normally be viewed as a fault in other beer styles. Clove, spice, banana, and sometimes bubblegum characters can all be found in these delightful beers. Belgian wheat beers, for example, often have a particularly distinct character from the addition of bitter orange peel and spices.

CLOUDY CHARACTER

The unique fermentation and serving technique give this style its particular character. Usually served cool and well carbonated, wheat beers are always conditioned in the bottle. This allows the yeast sediment to be gently roused when serving to produce a cloudy beer.

Wheat beers are easy to re-create at home due to the higher fermentation temperatures and wide range of acceptable flavors. They are also designed to be drunk when young, making them ideal quick brews.

Weissbier

Weissbier (white beer) originates from Bavaria. The name refers to the fact that it was lighter in color than other ales from the region.

Appearance Light straw to dark golden, with a thick, long-lasting head. Often served cloudy.

Taste A relatively low bitterness, often with notes of clove, banana, and vanilla.

Aroma Light hop aroma with citrus, banana, and clove characters, without being too overpowering.

Strength 4.3–5.6% ABV

There are several styles, mostly from Germany. For example, hefeweizen (yeast wheat) is unfiltered, cloudy, and has a low hop bitterness. Kristallweizen (crystal wheat), on the other hand, is filtered for greater clarity.

See pp186–191

Rye beer

Using rye in the mash adds a grainy flavor. Historically, rye was often used instead of barley in German brewing.

Appearance Light golden to dark, often with a hazy orange or red hue and a dense, long-lasting head.

Taste Grainy with a distinct, spicy rye flavor, similar to that found in pumpernickel or rye bread.

Aroma Light spicy rye aroma, often with clove and banana notes from the fermentation process.

Strength 4.5–6% ABV

Weizen yeasts fermented at lower temperatures give a complex banana and clove character to German rye beers.

American rye beers are strong and highly hopped. Spicy rye flavors are complemented by citrus hops and a fairly neutral yeast character.

See pp192–193

Witbier

A very old, almost lost style made popular again by Pierre Celis at Hoegaarden. Witbiers are spicy with moderate alcohol levels.

Appearance Very pale straw colors and always served cloudy with a dense, long-lasting head.

Taste Refreshingly crisp, tart, and spicy with orange fruit characters and a low hop aroma and bitterness.

Aroma The use of floral hops and spicy coriander gives a distinct, subtle aroma.

Strength 4.5–5.5% ABV

Belgian witbiers are generally spiced with coriander, orange, and other spices and herbs.

See pp194–195

Dark wheat beer

A strikingly dark brew with a more complex malt character than other styles of wheat beer.

Appearance Amber to deep brown, with a long-lasting, off-white head; served cloudy and well carbonated.

Taste Banana and clove flavors are present but tend to be dominated by sweet caramel notes from the roasted malts.

Aroma Moderate clove and banana aromas, with low noble-hop notes.

Strength 4.3–5.6% ABV

The German dunkelweizen style has distinctive banana and clove notes, with caramel malt flavors. It is lightly hopped with European noble hops.

American dark wheats are stronger and hoppier than German versions. Subtle malt flavors are complemented by citrus hops and a neutral yeast flavor.

See pp196–197

Originally brewed in Munich in 1907, this strong wheat beer is a rich, dark-amber brew with spicy clovelike flavors. It has a long-lasting, light-tan head when served.

WEIZENBOCK

ORIGINAL GRAVITY 1065 **EXPECTED FINAL GRAVITY** 1016 **TOTAL LIQUOR** 8.7 GALLONS (33.5 LITERS)

MAKES	READY TO DRINK	ESTIMATED ABV	BITTERNESS RATING	COLOR RATING
6 GALLONS (23 LITERS)	4 WEEKS	6.6%	19.8 IBU	28.3 EBC

FOR THE MASH

LIQUOR 4.2 gallons (16 liters)   **MASH TIME** 1 hr   **TEMPERATURE** 149°F (65°C)

Grain bill	Quantity
Wheat malt	8lb (3.6kg)
Munich malt	5lb 5oz (2.4kg)
Carawheat malt	9oz (250g)
Chocolate wheat malt	4¼oz (120g)

FOR THE BOIL

LIQUOR 7 gallons (27 liters)   **BOIL TIME** 1 hr 15 mins

Hops	Quantity	IBU	When to add
Saaz 4.2%	1⅔oz (48g)	19.8	At start of boil

Other			
Irish moss	1 tsp		For last 15 mins of boil

TO FERMENT

FERMENTATION 75°F (24°C)   **CONDITIONING** 3 weeks at 54°F (12°C)

Yeast
Wyeast 3056 Bavarian Wheat Blend

This unique-tasting Bavarian beer is dominated by banana and bubblegum flavors from the yeast. It is best served cloudy by rousing the yeast sediment when pouring.

WEISSBIER

ORIGINAL GRAVITY 1050   **EXPECTED FINAL GRAVITY** 1012   **TOTAL LIQUOR** 8.3 GALLONS (32 LITERS)

MAKES 6 GALLONS (23 LITERS)	READY TO DRINK 4 WEEKS	ESTIMATED ABV 5%	BITTERNESS RATING 15.3 IBU	COLOR RATING 6.3 EBC

FOR THE MASH

LIQUOR 3.2 gallons (12.5 liters)   **MASH TIME** 1 hr   **TEMPERATURE** 149°F (65°C)

Grain bill	Quantity
Wheat malt	6lb (2.7kg)
Pilsner malt	5lb (2.3kg)

FOR THE BOIL

LIQUOR 7 gallons (27 liters)   **BOIL TIME** 1 hr 10 mins

Hops	Quantity	IBU	When to add
Hallertauer Hersbrucker 3.5%	1oz (25g)	9.6	At start of boil
Saaz 4.2%	½oz (12g)	5.7	At start of boil
Other			
Irish moss	1 tsp		For last 15 mins of boil

TO FERMENT

FERMENTATION 72°F (22°C)   **CONDITIONING** 3 weeks at 54°F (12°C)

Yeast
Wyeast 3068 Weihenstephan Weizen

MALT EXTRACT VERSION

Add 6lb 10oz (3kg) **dried wheat malt extract** to 7 gallons (27 liters) water, bring to a boil, and add the hops as specified in the main recipe.

Originating from Goslar in Germany, the gose style combines lemony sourness, saltiness, and herbal flavors to make a deliciously refreshing summer beer.

GOSE

ORIGINAL GRAVITY 1038 **EXPECTED FINAL GRAVITY** 1005 **TOTAL LIQUOR** 7.7 GALLONS (29 LITERS)

MAKES 6 GALLONS (23 LITERS)	READY TO DRINK 3 WEEKS	ESTIMATED ABV 4.2%	BITTERNESS RATING 2.5 IBU	COLOR RATING 5.8 EBC

FOR THE MASH

LIQUOR 2.6 gallons (10 liters)   **MASH TIME** 1 hr   **TEMPERATURE** 147°F (64°C)

Grain bill	Quantity
Pilsner malt	4¾lb (2.15 kg)
Wheat malt	2¾lb (1.7kg)
Golden Naked Oats	9oz (250g)

FOR THE BOIL

LIQUOR 7 gallons (27 liters)   **BOIL TIME** 1 hr 15 mins

Hops	Quantity	IBU	When to add
Hersbrucker 3.5%	⅛oz (5g)	2.5	At start of boil

Other			
Irish moss	1 tsp		For last 15 mins of boil
Coriander seeds, lightly crushed	½oz (15g)		For last 10 mins of boil

TO FERMENT

FERMENTATION 90°F (32°C)   **CONDITIONING** 2 weeks at 50°F (10°C)

Yeast
Omega Yeast OYL57 Hothead

Bacteria	When to add
Lactobacillus	At start of fermentation

Other	
Sea salt, to taste (start with around ¾oz/20g)	After fermentation

This hazy, refreshing beer is packed with exuberant
citrus flavors and aromas, which are imparted by
the powerful American hops and yeast.

AMERICAN WHEAT BEER

ORIGINAL GRAVITY 1058 **EXPECTED FINAL GRAVITY** 1013 **TOTAL LIQUOR** 8.6 GALLONS (33 LITERS)

MAKES	READY TO DRINK	ESTIMATED ABV	BITTERNESS RATING	COLOR RATING
6 GALLONS (23 LITERS)	4 WEEKS	5.9%	25 IBU	9.1 EBC

FOR THE MASH

LIQUOR 3.8 gallons (14.5 liters)   **MASH TIME** 1 hr   **TEMPERATURE** 149°F (65°C)

Grain bill	Quantity
Wheat malt	6lb 10oz (3kg)
US domestic 2-row malt	5½lb (2.5kg)
Carapils malt	10½oz (300g)

FOR THE BOIL

LIQUOR 7 gallons (27 liters)   **BOIL TIME** 1 hr 10 mins

Hops	Quantity	IBU	When to add
Citra 13.8%	⅔oz (17g)	25.0	At start of boil
Citra 13.8%	1oz (26g)	0.0	At end of boil
Other			
Irish moss	1 tsp		For last 15 mins of boil

TO FERMENT

FERMENTATION 64°F (18°C)   **CONDITIONING** 3 weeks at 54°F (12°C)

Yeast
Wyeast 1010 American Wheat

MALT EXTRACT VERSION

Steep 10½oz (300g) **Carapils malt** in 7 gallons (27 liters)
water at 149°F (65°C) for 30 mins. Remove the malt, then
add 7lb 4oz (3.3kg) **dried wheat malt extract**, bring to a
boil, and add the hops as specified in the main recipe.

BREWER'S TIP

To increase the fruit flavors
from the yeast, try fermenting
the brew at the warmer
temperature of 72°F (22°C).

Tart and super refreshing, this is a modern take on a traditional German style that originates from Berlin. After pitching the *Lactobacillus*, be sure to wait 24 hours before pitching the yeast.

RASPBERRY MOSAIC BERLINER WEISSE

ORIGINAL GRAVITY 1035 **EXPECTED FINAL GRAVITY** 1007 **TOTAL LIQUOR** 7.5 GALLONS (28.5 LITERS)

MAKES	READY TO DRINK	ESTIMATED ABV	BITTERNESS RATING	COLOR RATING
6 GALLONS (23 LITERS)	3 WEEKS	3.7%	0 IBU	5.6 EBC

FOR THE MASH

LIQUOR 2.5 gallons (9.5 liters) **MASH TIME** 1 hr **TEMPERATURE** 153°F (67°C)

Grain bill	Quantity
Pilsner malt	5½lb (2.5 kg)
Wheat malt	2¾lb (1.25kg)

FOR THE BOIL

LIQUOR 7 gallons (27 liters) **BOIL TIME** 1 hr 15 mins

Other		
Irish moss	1 tsp	For last 15 mins of boil

TO FERMENT

FERMENTATION 95°F (35°C) **CONDITIONING** 2 weeks at 50°F (10°C)

Bacteria	Quantity	When to add
White Labs WLP672 Lactobacillus Brevis		At start of fermentation

Yeast
Reduce to 68°F (20°C) before pitching the yeast

Yeast Bay Sigmund's Voss Kveik		After 1 day of fermentation
Brettanomyces claussenii		After 1 day of fermentation

Other		
Raspberries, frozen	2¼lb (1kg)	After fermentation

BREWER'S TIP

Pitch the Lactobacillus first, then add the yeast 24 hours later.

Originating from Bavaria, this unusual beer combines a strong, spicy flavor from the rye malt with complex apple, pear, and banana notes from the yeast.

ROGGENBIER

ORIGINAL GRAVITY 1051 **EXPECTED FINAL GRAVITY** 1013 **TOTAL LIQUOR** 8.3 GALLONS (32 LITERS)

MAKES	READY TO DRINK	ESTIMATED ABV	BITTERNESS RATING	COLOR RATING
6 GALLONS (23 LITERS)	4 WEEKS	5%	14.6 IBU	30.9 EBC

FOR THE MASH

LIQUOR 3.2 gallons (12.25 liters) **MASH TIME** 1 hr **TEMPERATURE** 149°F (65°C)

Grain bill	Quantity
Rye malt	6lb 6oz (2.9kg)
Munich malt	3lb 8oz (1.6kg)
Crystal wheat malt	10½oz (300g)
Carafa special III	4¼oz (120g)

FOR THE BOIL

LIQUOR 7 gallons (27 liters) **BOIL TIME** 1 hr 15 mins

Hops	Quantity	IBU	When to add
Hallertauer Hersbrucker 3.5%	1oz (31g)	11.7	At start of boil
Hallertauer Hersbrucker 3.5%	½oz (15g)	2.8	For last 10 mins of boil
Tettnang 4.5%	½oz (15g)	0.0	At end of boil

Other			
Irish moss	1 tsp		For last 15 mins of boil

TO FERMENT

FERMENTATION 75°F (24°C) **CONDITIONING** 3 weeks at 54°F (12°C)

Yeast
Wyeast 3638 Bavarian Wheat

Light, crisp, and slightly spicy, this beer has refreshing citrus notes from the American hops, which are complemented by a clean finish from the German yeast.

RYE BEER

ORIGINAL GRAVITY 1056 EXPECTED FINAL GRAVITY 1013 TOTAL LIQUOR 8.4 GALLONS (32.5 LITERS)

MAKES 6 GALLONS (23 LITERS)	READY TO DRINK 4 WEEKS	ESTIMATED ABV 5.6%	BITTERNESS RATING 25.5 IBU	COLOR RATING 9.8 EBC

FOR THE MASH

LIQUOR 3.6 gallons (13.75 liters)   MASH TIME 1 hr   TEMPERATURE 149°F (65°C)

Grain bill	Quantity
Rye malt	6lb 10oz (3kg)
Pale malt	5½b (2.5kg)

FOR THE BOIL

LIQUOR 7 gallons (27 liters)   BOIL TIME 1 hr 10 mins

Hops	Quantity	IBU	When to add
Chinook 13.3%	⅔oz (18g)	25.5	At start of boil
Amarillo 5%	1¾oz (50g)	0.0	At end of boil

Other			
Irish moss	1 tsp		For last 15 mins of boil

TO FERMENT

FERMENTATION 64°F (18°C)   CONDITIONING 3 weeks at 54°F (12°C)

Yeast
Wyeast 2565 Kölsch

Hops	Quantity	When to add
Amarillo 5%	1oz (25g)	After 4 days, leave for about 1 week

This is a classic, Belgian-style cloudy beer. A spicy coriander flavor mixes with complex banana and orange notes to give this "white beer" its distinct character.

WITBIER

ORIGINAL GRAVITY 1045 **EXPECTED FINAL GRAVITY** 1011 **TOTAL LIQUOR** 8.2 GALLONS (31.5 LITERS)

MAKES	READY TO DRINK	ESTIMATED ABV	BITTERNESS RATING	COLOR RATING
6 GALLONS (23 LITERS)	4 WEEKS	4.5%	15.3 IBU	7.8 EBC

FOR THE MASH

LIQUOR 3 gallons (11.5 liters) **MASH TIME** 1 hr **TEMPERATURE** 149°F (65°C)

Grain bill	Quantity
Wheat malt	5lb (2.3kg)
Pale malt	5lb (2.3kg)

FOR THE BOIL

LIQUOR 7 gallons (27 liters) **BOIL TIME** 1 hr 10 mins

Hops	Quantity	IBU	When to add
Saaz 4.2%	1oz (32g)	15.3	At start of boil

Other			
Irish moss	1 tsp		For last 15 mins of boil
Curaçao bitter orange peel	1oz (25g)		For last 10 mins of boil
Coriander seeds, lightly crushed	1oz (25g)		For last 10 mins of boil

TO FERMENT

FERMENTATION 75°F (24°C) **CONDITIONING** 3 weeks at 54°F (12°C)

Yeast
Wyeast 3944 Belgian Witbier

MALT EXTRACT VERSION

Add 6lb (2.7kg) **dried wheat malt extract** to 7 gallons (27 liters) water, bring to a boil, and add the hops and other ingredients as specified in the main recipe.

BREWER'S TIP

Ensure you have plenty of space at the top of the fermenter since this yeast creates a large krausen during fermentation.

This addictive, creamy, German wheat beer has a complex malt character that fuses well with the mix of fruity flavors imparted by the blended yeast strain.

DUNKELWEIZEN

ORIGINAL GRAVITY 1056 **EXPECTED FINAL GRAVITY** 1014 **TOTAL LIQUOR** 8.4 GALLONS (32.5 LITERS)

MAKES 6 GALLONS (23 LITERS)	READY TO DRINK 4 WEEKS	ESTIMATED ABV 5.6%	BITTERNESS RATING 15.3 IBU	COLOR RATING 29.5 EBC

FOR THE MASH

LIQUOR 3.5 gallons (13.5 liters)   **MASH TIME** 1 hr   **TEMPERATURE** 149°F (65°C)

Grain bill	Quantity
Wheat malt	6lb (2.7kg)
Munich malt	5lb (2.3kg)
Caramunich III	10½oz (300g)
Special B	10½oz (300g)

FOR THE BOIL

LIQUOR 7 gallons (27 liters)   **BOIL TIME** 1 hr 10 mins

Hops	Quantity	IBU	When to add
Tettnang 4.5%	1oz (32g)	15.3	At start of boil
Other			
Irish moss	1 tsp		For last 15 mins of boil

TO FERMENT

FERMENTATION 72°F (22°C)   **CONDITIONING** 3 weeks at 54°F (12°C)

Yeast
Wyeast 3056 Bavarian Wheat Blend

More like an ale than a traditional wheat beer, this dark and malty brew has the distinct flavor and character of wheat but with a hoppy, citrus aroma and flavor.

DARK WHEAT BEER

ORIGINAL GRAVITY 1064 **EXPECTED FINAL GRAVITY** 1015 **TOTAL LIQUOR** 8.7 GALLONS (33.5 LITERS)

MAKES	READY TO DRINK	ESTIMATED ABV	BITTERNESS RATING	COLOR RATING
6 GALLONS (23 LITERS)	6 WEEKS	6.5%	44 IBU	28.8 EBC

FOR THE MASH

LIQUOR 4.2 gallons (16.25 liters)   **MASH TIME** 1 hr   **TEMPERATURE** 149°F (65°C)

Grain bill	Quantity
Vienna malt	6lb 10oz (3kg)
Wheat malt	5lb 12oz (2.6kg)
Biscuit malt	1lb 2oz (500g)
Crystal wheat	10½oz (300g)
Carafa special I	3½oz (100g)

FOR THE BOIL

LIQUOR 7 gallons (27 liters)   **BOIL TIME** 1 hr 10 mins

Hops	Quantity	IBU	When to add
Magnum 11%	1⅓oz (40g)	44.1	At start of boil
Willamette 6.3%	¾oz (24g)	0.0	At end of boil

Other			
Irish moss	1 tsp		For last 15 mins of boil

TO FERMENT

FERMENTATION 64°F (18°C)   **CONDITIONING** 5 weeks at 54°F (12°C)

Yeast
Wyeast 2565 Kölsch

MIXED STYLES

The beers in this category can't be neatly defined as a lager, ale, or wheat beer—although they may share certain qualities and brewing techniques.

Included in this group are hybrid beers, which often use a combination of lager and ale fermentation methods. Kölsch (see p201), for example, is brewed as an ale with top-fermenting yeast but is conditioned in cool conditions and has a clean, lager finish. Californian Common (see p202), on the other hand, is produced with lager yeast but is fermented at warmer ale temperatures.

GET CREATIVE

For the creative home brewer, herb, spice, fruit, and even vegetable beers are perfect for experimentation. Use the recipes in this section as a starting point from which to build your own repertoire of wild and wonderful brews. As long as you pick complementary flavors and use appropriate quantities, there's no reason you can't produce an exciting and delicious beer from any number of natural ingredients.

THREE KEYS TO SUCCESS

■ Add fruit to the fermenter after primary fermentation is complete—when the presence of alcohol will reduce the chance of bacterial contamination—rather than to the boiler, because a lot of the fruit character will be lost if the fruit is boiled.

■ Add herbs and spices to the boil to allow them to infuse, but only for a few minutes at the end. If boiled for too long, the delicate flavors and aromas will be cooked away and replaced by bitter, or even astringent, characteristics. Herbs and spices can also be added directly to the fermenter after primary fermentation is complete.

■ Less is more when it comes to quantities—a subtle herb, spice, fruit, or vegetable character is usually more desirable than an overly assertive flavor.

Light hybrids

These beers use bottom-fermenting lager yeasts but are fermented at ale temperatures to create a full-bodied ale flavor with a clean lager finish.

Appearance Depends on the style but often very pale, crystal clear, and with a persistent white head.

Taste Depends on the style but usually clean with low bitterness and a dry finish.

Aroma Typically neutral aroma with a low malt and hop presence.

Strength 3.8–5.6% ABV

Cream ales are popular American hybrid beers. They are light, clean, and very refreshing.

Kölsch is light, hoppy, clear, and brewed using top-fermenting yeast. The name is protected and restricted to about 20 breweries in and around Cologne, Germany.

See pp200-201

Amber hybrids

Similar to light hybrids but brewed with roasted malts for greater depth of flavor, these light brown beers are also known as bitter lagers.

Appearance Light brown to deep copper, usually very clear with good head retention.

Taste Fairly bitter and malty, with a clean, crisp finish.

Aroma Moderately hoppy with subtle malt aromas, depending on the style.

Strength 4.5–5.5% ABV

Altbiers from northern Germany—and Düsseldorf in particular—are typical amber hybrids. The name ("old beer") refers to the traditional brewing process in which ale yeast is fermented at cool, lager temperatures.

See pp202–205

Herb and spice beers

Use only small amounts of herbs and spices when experimenting with different flavors.

Appearance Usually clear, with the color varying greatly, depending on the nature of the ingredients.

Taste Generally dry with a subtle character from the herbs and spices.

Aroma Can have a mild hoppiness, although the herbs will provide the dominant aroma.

Strength 4–6% ABV

Fraoch, meaning "heather" in Gaelic, is an ancient and unique style that has been brewed in Scotland for thousands of years.

See pp206–209

Fruit and vegetable beers

Fruit and vegetables impart depth of flavor and add great character to a beer.

Appearance Depends on the fruit or vegetables used but often slightly hazy.

Taste The particular fruit or vegetables added will provide the dominant flavors, although this should be subtle and balanced by hop bitterness.

Aroma A light hop and malt aroma should perfectly complement the fruit or vegetable character.

Strength 4–6% ABV

Fruit wheat beers and cherry lambics are popular Belgian styles. Peach and raspberry beers are also common.

Pumpkin beer is a fall favorite in the US; pale ale brewed with chile pepper is also popular.

See pp210-215

A classic American ale, this beer is light, crisp, and very refreshing on a warm summer's day. The subtle citrus aromas are perfectly balanced by a clean, neutral finish.

CREAM ALE

ORIGINAL GRAVITY 1055 **EXPECTED FINAL GRAVITY** 1014 **TOTAL LIQUOR** 8.4 GALLONS (32.5 LITERS)

MAKES 6 GALLONS (23 LITERS)	READY TO DRINK 4 WEEKS	ESTIMATED ABV 5.5%	BITTERNESS RATING 19.8 IBU	COLOR RATING 9.6 EBC

FOR THE MASH

LIQUOR 3.6 gallons (13.75 liters) **MASH TIME** 1 hr **TEMPERATURE** 149°F (65°C)

Grain bill	Quantity
Pale malt	11lb (5kg)
Flaked corn (maize)	1lb 2oz (500g)

FOR THE BOIL

LIQUOR 7 gallons (27 liters) **BOIL TIME** 1 hr 10 mins

Hops	Quantity	IBU	When to add
Centennial 8.5%	¾oz (22g)	19.8	At start of boil
Mount Hood 4.5%	1¼oz (33g)	0.0	At end of boil

Other			
Irish moss	1 tsp		For last 15 mins of boil

TO FERMENT

FERMENTATION 64°F (18°C) **CONDITIONING** 3 weeks at 54°F (12°C)

Yeast
Wyeast 2112 California Lager

A German speciality brew, Kölsch is top-fermented like an ale but conditioned at low temperatures like a lager. It has a subtle, floral hoppiness and a clean character.

KÖLSCH

ORIGINAL GRAVITY 1046 **EXPECTED FINAL GRAVITY** 1011 **TOTAL LIQUOR** 8.2 GALLONS (31.5 LITERS)

MAKES 6 GALLONS (23 LITERS)	READY TO DRINK 4 WEEKS	ESTIMATED ABV 4.6%	BITTERNESS RATING 25 IBU	COLOR RATING 7.2 EBC

FOR THE MASH

LIQUOR 2.9 gallons (11.25 liters)   **MASH TIME** 1 hr   **TEMPERATURE** 149°F (65°C)

Grain bill	Quantity
Pilsner malt	8lb 13oz (4kg)
Carapils malt	1lb 2oz (500g)

FOR THE BOIL

LIQUOR 7 gallons (27 liters)   **BOIL TIME** 1 hr 10 mins

Hops	Quantity	IBU	When to add
Spalt Select 4.5%	1½oz (44g)	22.8	At start of boil
Tettnang 4.5%	¾oz (22g)	2.2	For last 5 mins of boil
Tettnang 4.5%	1½oz (44g)	0.0	At end of boil

Other			
Irish moss	1 tsp		For last 15 mins of boil

TO FERMENT

FERMENTATION 64°F (18°C)   **CONDITIONING** 3 weeks at 54°F (12°C)

Yeast
Wyeast 2565 Kölsch

MALT EXTRACT VERSION

Steep 1lb 2oz (500g) **Carapils malt** in 7 gallons (27 liters) water at 149°F (65°C) for 30 mins. Remove the malt, then add 5½lb (2.5kg) **dried extra-light malt extract**, bring to a boil, and add the hops as specified in the main recipe.

This is an American-style amber ale with a clean, lagerlike finish. The woody, minty hop aromas and flavors come from the German Northern Brewer hops.

CALIFORNIAN COMMON

ORIGINAL GRAVITY 1052 **EXPECTED FINAL GRAVITY** 1016 **TOTAL LIQUOR** 8.3 GALLONS (32 LITERS)

MAKES 6 GALLONS (23 LITERS)	READY TO DRINK 6 WEEKS	ESTIMATED ABV 4.8%	BITTERNESS RATING 40.5 IBU	COLOR RATING 21.8 EBC

FOR THE MASH

LIQUOR 3.4 gallons (13 liters)   **MASH TIME** 1 hr   **TEMPERATURE** 149°F (65°C)

Grain bill	Quantity
Pale malt	8lb 6oz (3.8kg)
Vienna malt	2¼lb (1kg)
Medium crystal malt	10½oz (300g)
Chocolate malt	1¾oz (50g)

FOR THE BOIL

LIQUOR 7 gallons (27 liters)   **BOIL TIME** 1 hr 10 mins

Hops	Quantity	IBU	When to add
Northern Brewer 8%	1½oz (41g)	36.3	At start of boil
Northern Brewer 8%	½oz (14g)	4.2	For last 10 mins of boil
Northern Brewer 8%	1½oz (41g)	0.0	At end of boil

Other			
Irish moss	1 tsp		For last 15 mins of boil

TO FERMENT

FERMENTATION 64°F (18°C)   **CONDITIONING** 5 weeks at 54°F (12°C)

Yeast
Wyeast 2112 California Lager

This is a fine example of a typical altbier, or "old beer,"
from Germany. It is a clean, dark brown, relatively bitter
beer with a caramel maltiness.

NORTH GERMAN ALTBIER

ORIGINAL GRAVITY 1048 **EXPECTED FINAL GRAVITY** 1012 **TOTAL LIQUOR** 8.3 GALLONS (32 LITERS)

MAKES 6 GALLONS (23 LITERS)	READY TO DRINK 8 WEEKS	ESTIMATED ABV 4.8%	BITTERNESS RATING 34.9 IBU	COLOR RATING 26.5 EBC

FOR THE MASH

LIQUOR 3.4 gallons (13 liters)   **MASH TIME** 1 hr   **TEMPERATURE** 149°F (65°C)

Grain bill	Quantity
Pilsner malt	4½lb (2kg)
Pale malt	4½lb (2kg)
Caramunich III	1lb 2oz (500g)
Carapils	10½oz (300g)
Carafa special III	2oz (60g)

FOR THE BOIL

LIQUOR 7 gallons (27 liters)   **BOIL TIME** 1 hr 10 mins

Hops	Quantity	IBU	When to add
Magnum 11%	1oz (28g)	34.7	At start of boil

Other			
Irish moss	1 tsp		For last 15 mins of boil

TO FERMENT

FERMENTATION 54°F (12°C)   **CONDITIONING** 7 weeks at 37°F (3°C)

Yeast
Wyeast 1007 German Ale

MALT EXTRACT VERSION
Steep 1lb 2oz (500g) **Caramunich III**, 10½oz (300g)
Carapils malt, and 2oz (60g) **Carafa special III** in 7 gallons
(27 liters) water at 149°F (65°C) for 30 mins. Remove
the malt, then add 5½lb (2.5kg) **dried extra-light malt
extract**, bring to a boil, and add the hops as specified in
the main recipe.

Düsseldorf Altbier is stronger and more bitter than altbiers brewed in other areas. Cool fermentation and extended lagering produce a smooth, silky ale.

DÜSSELDORF ALTBIER

ORIGINAL GRAVITY 1053 **EXPECTED FINAL GRAVITY** 1013 **TOTAL LIQUOR** 8.3 GALLONS (32 LITERS)

MAKES	READY TO	ESTIMATED	BITTERNESS	COLOR
6 GALLONS	DRINK	ABV	RATING	RATING
(23 LITERS)	8 WEEKS	5.3%	49.6 IBU	22.1 EBC

FOR THE MASH

LIQUOR 3.4 gallons (13 liters)　　**MASH TIME** 1 hr　　**TEMPERATURE** 149°F (65°C)

Grain bill	Quantity
Pilsner malt	10lb 9oz (4.8kg)
Light crystal malt	12oz (350g)
Black malt	2½oz (70g)

FOR THE BOIL

LIQUOR 7 gallons (27 liters)　　**BOIL TIME** 1 hr 10 mins

Hops	Quantity	IBU	When to add
Spalt Select 4.5%	3¼oz (93g)	45.3	At start of boil
Spalt Select 4.5 %	1½oz (46g)	4.4	For last 5 mins of boil
Spalt Select 4.5%	1¾oz (50g)	0.0	At end of boil

Other			
Irish moss	1 tsp		For last 15 mins of boil

TO FERMENT

FERMENTATION 64°F (18°C)　　**CONDITIONING** 7 weeks at 37°F (3°C)

Yeast
Wyeast 1275 Thames Valley Ale

MALT EXTRACT VERSION`

Steep 12oz (350g) **light crystal malt** and 2½oz (70g) **black malt** in 7 gallons (27 liters) water at 149°F (65°C) for 30 mins. Remove the malt, then add 6lb 10oz (3kg) **dried extra-light malt extract**, bring to a boil, and add the hops as specified in the main recipe.

The flavors in this unusual beer work surprisingly well together. With notes of spice and citrus, and a hoppy aroma, it is a great beer to enjoy with spicy food.

SPICED CORIANDER AND LIME BEER

ORIGINAL GRAVITY 1050 **EXPECTED FINAL GRAVITY** 1011 **TOTAL LIQUOR** 8.3 GALLONS (32 LITERS)

MAKES 6 GALLONS (23 LITERS)	READY TO DRINK 4 WEEKS	ESTIMATED ABV 5.1%	BITTERNESS RATING 37.1 IBU	COLOR RATING 9 EBC

FOR THE MASH

LIQUOR 3.3 gallons (12.5 liters) **MASH TIME** 1 hr **TEMPERATURE** 149°F (65°C)

Grain bill	Quantity
Pale malt	8lb 13oz (4kg)
Carapils	1lb 2oz (500g)
Wheat malt	1lb 2oz (500g)

FOR THE BOIL

LIQUOR 7 gallons (27 liters) **BOIL TIME** 1 hr 10 mins

Hops	Quantity	IBU	When to add
Magnum 16%	⅔oz (20g)	35.4	At start of boil
Liberty 4.5%	⅓oz (10g)	1.7	For last 10 mins of boil
Liberty 4.5%	1oz (30g)	0.0	At end of boil

Other			
Irish moss	1 tsp		For last 15 mins of boil
Coriander seeds, crushed	1oz (25g)		For last 10 mins of boil

TO FERMENT

FERMENTATION 64°F (18°C) **CONDITIONING** 2 weeks at 54°F (12°C)

Yeast
White Labs WLP001 California Ale

Hops/other	Quantity	When to add
Styrian Golding Bobek	1¾oz (50g)	After 4 days, leave for about 1 week
Dried lemongrass, crushed	4 stalks	As above
Dried kaffir lime leaves	¼oz (5g)	As above
Fresh ginger, grated	1¾oz (50g)	As above

Traditionally brewed using only spruce tips and molasses, this modern version retains the resinous character of the spruce but results in a more well-rounded ale.

SPRUCE BEER

ORIGINAL GRAVITY 1051 **EXPECTED FINAL GRAVITY** 1014 **TOTAL LIQUOR** 8.3 GALLONS (32 LITERS)

MAKES	READY TO DRINK	ESTIMATED ABV	BITTERNESS RATING	COLOR RATING
6 GALLONS (23 LITERS)	6 WEEKS	4.8%	25 IBU	15.5 EBC

FOR THE MASH

LIQUOR 3.3 gallons (12.75 liters) **MASH TIME** 1 hr **TEMPERATURE** 149°F (65°C)

Grain bill	Quantity
Pale malt	9lb 11oz (4.4kg)
Caramalt	1lb 2oz (500g)
Crystal wheat	7oz (200g)

FOR THE BOIL

LIQUOR 7 gallons (27 liters) **BOIL TIME** 1 hr 10 mins

Hops	Quantity	IBU	When to add
Magnum 16%	½oz (14g)	25.0	At start of boil
Magnum 16%	¼oz (7g)	0.0	At end of boil

Other			
Spruce tips	5½oz (150g)		At start of boil
Irish moss	1 tsp		For last 15 mins of boil

TO FERMENT

FERMENTATION 64°F (18°C) **CONDITIONING** 4 weeks at 54°F (12°C)

Yeast
White Labs WLP013 London Ale

Hops	Quantity	When to add
Apollo 19.5%	1¾oz (50g)	After 4 days, leave for about 1 week

This cloudy, spicy brew is similar to a Belgian wheat beer but has a dry, honey finish. Clove, orange, and spicy coriander flavors make this a unique and refreshing beer.

SPICED HONEY BEER

ORIGINAL GRAVITY 1051 **EXPECTED FINAL GRAVITY** 1009 **TOTAL LIQUOR** 8.3 GALLONS (32 LITERS)

MAKES 6 GALLONS (23 LITERS)	READY TO DRINK 4 WEEKS	ESTIMATED ABV 5.6%	BITTERNESS RATING 11.6 IBU	COLOR RATING 9.1 EBC

FOR THE MASH

LIQUOR 2.9 gallons (11 liters)   **MASH TIME** 1 hr   **TEMPERATURE** 149°F (65°C)

Grain bill	Quantity
Pale malt	9lb 11oz (4.4kg)

FOR THE BOIL

LIQUOR 7 gallons (27 liters)   **BOIL TIME** 1 hr 10 mins

Hops	Quantity	IBU	When to add
Hallertauer Hersbrucker 4.1%	¾oz (22g)	10.6	At start of boil
Hallertauer Hersbrucker 4.1%	¼oz (5g)	0.9	For last 5 mins of boil
Hallertauer Hersbrucker 4.1%	¼oz (6g)	0.1	For last 1 min of boil

Other			
Irish moss	1 tsp		For last 15 mins of boil
Coriander seeds, crushed	1¼oz (38g)		For last 10 mins of boil
Curaçao bitter orange peel	½oz (16g)		For last 10 mins of boil
Honey	1lb 2oz (500g)		For last 10 mins of boil

TO FERMENT

FERMENTATION 75°F (24°C)   **CONDITIONING** 3 weeks at 54°F (12°C)

Yeast
Wyeast 3068 Weihenstephan Weizen

MALT EXTRACT VERSION

Add 6lb (2.7kg) **dried extra-light malt extract** to 7 gallons (27 liters) water, bring to a boil, and add the hops as specified in the main recipe.

This brew is more like an ale with added ginger than a traditional ginger beer. Its distinct spicy character is complemented by the citrus qualities of the Galaxy hops.

GINGER BEER

ORIGINAL GRAVITY 1045 EXPECTED FINAL GRAVITY 1011 TOTAL LIQUOR 8.5 GALLONS (32.5 LITERS)

MAKES	READY TO DRINK	ESTIMATED ABV	BITTERNESS RATING	COLOR RATING
6 GALLONS (23 LITERS)	4 WEEKS	4.5%	25.1 IBU	6.3 EBC

FOR THE MASH

LIQUOR 3.6 gallons (13.75 liters)   MASH TIME 1 hr   TEMPERATURE 149°F (65°C)

Grain bill	Quantity
US domestic 2-row malt	7lb 11oz (3.5kg)
Flaked corn (maize)	2¼lb (1kg)

FOR THE BOIL

LIQUOR 7 gallons (27 liters)   BOIL TIME 1 hr 10 mins

Hops	Quantity	IBU	When to add
Galaxy 14.4%	½oz (14g)	22.9	At start of boil
Galaxy 14.4%	¼oz (7g)	2.1	For last 5 mins of boil
Galaxy 14.4%	⅔oz (20g)	0.0	At end of boil

Other			
Irish moss	1 tsp		For last 15 mins of boil
Freshly grated ginger	5½oz (150g)		For last 5 mins of boil

TO FERMENT

FERMENTATION 64°F (18°C)   CONDITIONING 3 weeks at 54°F (12°C)

Yeast
Wyeast 1028 London Ale

BREWER'S TIP

To give the finished beer a really intense, fiery flavor, add more freshly grated ginger—up to 10½oz (300g)—to the boil.

Adding raspberries during fermentation makes this Belgian-style wheat beer simply irresistible. It's a great summer brew that is sure to convert non-beer drinkers!

RASPBERRY WHEAT BEER

ORIGINAL GRAVITY 1050 **EXPECTED FINAL GRAVITY** 1012 **TOTAL LIQUOR** 8.3 GALLONS (32 LITERS)

MAKES 6 GALLONS (23 LITERS)	READY TO DRINK 4 WEEKS	ESTIMATED ABV 5.1%	BITTERNESS RATING 15.3 IBU	COLOR RATING 7.2 EBC

FOR THE MASH

LIQUOR 3.2 gallons (12.5 liters)   **MASH TIME** 1 hr   **TEMPERATURE** 149°F (65°C)

Grain bill	Quantity
US domestic 2-row malt	6lb (2.7kg)
Wheat malt	5lb (2.3kg)

FOR THE BOIL

LIQUOR 7 gallons (27 liters)   **BOIL TIME** 1 hr 10 mins

Hops	Quantity	IBU	When to add
Challenger 7%	⅔oz (20g)	15.0	At start of boil
Other			
Irish moss	1 tsp		For last 15 mins of boil

TO FERMENT

FERMENTATION 72°F (22°C)   **CONDITIONING** 2 weeks at 54°F (12°C)

Yeast
Wyeast 1010 American Wheat

Other	Quantity	When to add
Raspberries	5½lb (2.5kg)	After 2 days, leave for about 1 week

MALT EXTRACT VERSION

Add 6lb 10oz (3kg) **dried light malt extract** to 7 gallons (27 liters) water, bring to a boil, and add the hops as specified in the main recipe.

BREWER'S TIP

Substitute frozen raspberries for fresh ones if you prefer—they work just as well and are often less expensive.

The fresh fruit in this delicious and refreshing summer beer adds a subtle, dry strawberry flavor that is not as sweet or overpowering as you might expect.

STRAWBERRY BEER

ORIGINAL GRAVITY 1044 **EXPECTED FINAL GRAVITY** 1010 **TOTAL LIQUOR** 8.6 GALLONS (33 LITERS)

MAKES	READY TO DRINK	ESTIMATED ABV	BITTERNESS RATING	COLOR RATING
6 GALLONS (23 LITERS)	4 WEEKS	4.4%	18.4 IBU	8 EBC

FOR THE MASH

LIQUOR 3.8 gallons (14.5 liters)   **MASH TIME** 1 hr   **TEMPERATURE** 149°F (65°C)

Grain bill	Quantity
US domestic 2-row malt	7½lb (3.4kg)
Munich malt	1lb 10oz (750g)
Torrified wheat malt	9oz (250g)

FOR THE BOIL

LIQUOR 7 gallons (27 liters)   **BOIL TIME** 1 hr 10 mins

Hops	Quantity	IBU	When to add
Challenger 7%	⅔oz (20g)	16.2	At start of boil
Styrian Golding Celeia	⅓oz (10g)	2.2	For last 10 mins of boil
Styrian Golding Celeia	1oz (30g)	0.0	At end of boil

Other			
Irish moss	1 tsp		For last 15 mins of boil

TO FERMENT

FERMENTATION 64°F (18°C)   **CONDITIONING** 2 weeks at 54°F (12°C)

Yeast
White Labs WLP001 California Ale

Hops	Quantity	When to add
Strawberries	7lb 11oz (3.5kg)	After 4 days, leave for about 1 week

The kiwi fruit in this New Zealand–style witbier lends citrus notes to the brew and gives it a striking twist. The complex fruit flavors are unusual yet satisfying.

KIWI WHEAT BEER

ORIGINAL GRAVITY 1055 **EXPECTED FINAL GRAVITY** 1013 **TOTAL LIQUOR** 8.5 GALLONS (32.5 LITERS)

MAKES 6 GALLONS (23 LITERS)	READY TO DRINK 6 WEEKS	ESTIMATED ABV 5.5%	BITTERNESS RATING 22.4 IBU	COLOR RATING 7.7 EBC

FOR THE MASH

LIQUOR 3.6 gallons (13.75 liters)   **MASH TIME** 1 hr   **TEMPERATURE** 149°F (65°C)

Grain bill	Quantity
US domestic 2-row malt	6lb 10oz (3kg)
Wheat malt	5½lb (2.5kg)

FOR THE BOIL

LIQUOR 7 gallons (27 liters)   **BOIL TIME** 1 hr 10 mins

Hops	Quantity	IBU	When to add
Challenger 7%	1oz (30g)	22.4	At start of boil
Styrian Golding Celeia 5.5%	⅔oz (20g)	0.0	At end of boil

Other	Quantity		When to add
Irish moss	1 tsp		For last 15 mins of boil
Coriander seeds, crushed	1oz (25g)		For last 5 mins of boil

TO FERMENT

FERMENTATION 72°F (22°C)   **CONDITIONING** 4 weeks at 54°F (12°C)

Yeast
White Labs WLP729 Sweet Mead

Other	Quantity	When to add
Kiwi fruit, peeled and chopped	3lb 3oz (1.5kg)	After 4 days, leave for about 1 week

MALT EXTRACT VERSION

Add 6lb 3oz (2.8kg) **dried light malt extract** to 7 gallons (27 liters) water, bring to a boil, and add the hops and other ingredients as specified in the main recipe.

Traditionally brewed in colonial America as a cheap, local alternative to malt beers, this seasonal ale is subtly spiced to complement the distinct pumpkin character.

PUMPKIN ALE

ORIGINAL GRAVITY 1050 **EXPECTED FINAL GRAVITY** 1012 **TOTAL LIQUOR** 8.3 GALLONS (32 LITERS)

MAKES 6 GALLONS (23 LITERS)	READY TO DRINK 6 WEEKS	ESTIMATED ABV 5.2%	BITTERNESS RATING 22.8 IBU	COLOR RATING 15.7 EBC

FOR THE MASH

LIQUOR 3.2 gallons (12.5 liters)   **MASH TIME** 1 hr   **TEMPERATURE** 149°F (65°C)

Grain bill	Quantity
Pale malt	7½lb (3.4kg)
Munich malt	2¼lb (1kg)
Wheat malt	1lb 2oz (500g)
Special B	3½oz (100g)

1 large pumpkin (approx 22lb/10kg), roasted for 1 hr, then cut into cubes and added to the mash with the grains

FOR THE BOIL

LIQUOR 7 gallons (27 liters)   **BOIL TIME** 1 hr 10 mins

Hops	Quantity	IBU	When to add
Magnum 16%	½oz (12g)	21.8	At start of boil
Hallertauer Mittelfrüh 5%	⅓oz (9g)	1.0	For last 5 mins of boil

Other			
Irish moss	1 tsp		For last 15 mins of boil
Cinnamon stick	1 stick		For last 5 mins of boil
Ground ginger	½ tsp		For last 5 mins of boil
Vanilla bean	¾in (2cm) piece		For last 5 mins of boil
Whole cloves, crushed	2 cloves		For last 5 mins of boil

TO FERMENT

FERMENTATION 64°F (18°C)   **CONDITIONING** 5 weeks at 54°F (12°C)

Yeast
White Labs WLP001 California Ale

Before the use of hops, nettles were used to flavor beer.
This brew has the best of both worlds—an earthy spiciness
from the nettles and floral, citrus notes from the hops.

NETTLE BEER

ORIGINAL GRAVITY 1041 **EXPECTED FINAL GRAVITY** 1010 **TOTAL LIQUOR** 8.1 GALLONS (31 LITERS)

MAKES 6 GALLONS (23 LITERS)	READY TO DRINK 4 WEEKS	ESTIMATED ABV 4%	BITTERNESS RATING 25 IBU	COLOR RATING 9.3 EBC

FOR THE MASH

LIQUOR 2.5 gallons (10 liters)   **MASH TIME** 1 hr   **TEMPERATURE** 149°F (65°C)

Grain bill	Quantity
Pale malt	6lb 10oz (3kg)
Munich malt	2¼lb (1kg)

FOR THE BOIL

LIQUOR 7 gallons (27 liters)   **BOIL TIME** 1 hr 10 mins

Hops	Quantity	IBU	When to add
Fuggle 4.5%	1¼oz (38g)	20.1	At start of boil
Willamette 6.3%	⅔oz (19g)	4.9	For last 10 mins of boil
Styrian Golding Celeia 5.5%	⅔oz (19g)	0.0	At end of boil

Other		
Freshly picked nettle tops	3½oz (100g)	At start of boil
Irish moss	1 tsp	For last 15 mins of boil

FERMENT

FERMENTATION 64°F (18°C)   **CONDITIONING** 3 weeks at 54°F (12°C)

Yeast
Wyeast 1275 Thames Valley Ale

CREATE YOUR OWN RECIPES

We all want to make unique beers that we can call our own—it's one of the reasons that many people begin home brewing. Starting off can be daunting, so follow these simple guidelines and example recipe to get you on your way.

HOW TO WRITE A RECIPE
The basic steps to producing your own beer recipe are as follows:

1 PICK A STYLE
Although it's tempting to try to create the Next Big Thing from the start, it's often best to stick to tried-and-true styles for your first few batches. Do add your own twist, but be aware that being too ambitious too soon can lead to disaster.

2 LOOK UP A STYLE'S GUIDELINES
Guidelines for each beer style can be found online in the Beer Judge Certification Program (BJCP) Style Guidelines. This will provide you with ranges to set your gravities, bitterness, and color (see below) and will also provide an idea of which sort of ingredients will help you achieve them, such as whether to use pale or dark malt.

3 SET PARAMETERS USING BREWING SOFTWARE
There are three main parameters that will determine how much of each ingredient to put in your beer. These are gravity (original and final), bitterness, and color. Certain ingredients or parts of the brewing process determine the final value for each parameter. The best way to get the calculations for your recipe right is by using brewing software (see p219).

Gravity
There are two measurements for gravity: original gravity (OG) and final gravity (FG); the difference between these values will help you determine alcohol content (or alcohol by volume/ABV; see p63). Original gravity is fairly easy to estimate, as it will be the total volume of the beer produced and the amount of fermentable ingredients (grain, malt extract, and/or sugar) in the recipe. Check pp22–25 for more information about different malts, adjuncts, and sugars.

Predicting final gravity is a little more complicated. First, you need to know how the grain type, mash temperature, pH, and grain:water ratio will affect the type of sugars created and how fermentable the wort is. Then the fermentation process itself needs to be considered, since the temperature, yeast strain, pitch rates, and starting oxygen will all have an impact.

The final gravity will determine your beer's mouthfeel and its balance of sweetness and dryness. The lower the final gravity, the less sweet a beer will taste. If the final gravity is too low, the beer may taste thin, bland, and watery, especially at lower ABVs.

Bitterness
Measured in IBU (International Bitterness Units), bitterness comes from your hop additions—the alpha acid percentage of your hops and the amount of time they are boiled. Bitterness balances the alcohol and sweetness in a beer. Note that any dry hops added after the boil will have a major influence only on the flavor and aroma of the beer and will have little impact on its bitterness. Check pp26–29 for more information about different hops.

Color
Measured in EBC (European brewing convention), SRM (Standard Reference Method), or Lovibond, color is determined by the malt used in the mash. The darker the malt that you use, the darker your beer will be in color and the higher its EBC value. Your choice of malt will also affect your beer's flavor and final gravity (certain malts contain more complex sugars that are harder for yeast to convert). Check pp24–25 for more information about different ingredients' effect on color.

4 BREW!
Once these parameters are all set and your software is calculating the correct ABV, color, and bitterness, you should be good to go.

EXAMPLE RECIPE—TROPICAL STOUT

This example recipe will help give you an idea of how to get from the BJCP guidelines to finished recipe. BJCP describes Tropical Stout as sweet and fruity with roast flavors, a medium-full mouthfeel, and a dark color with good head retention. Characteristic ingredients given include both dark and pale malts, hops for bitterness, and a warm-fermented lager yeast. The ingredients in the recipe below have been chosen on this basis.

A dark, sweet, moderately fruity, moderately strong ale with smooth roast flavors without a burnt harshness.

TROPICAL STOUT

ORIGINAL GRAVITY 1063   **EXPECTED FINAL GRAVITY** 1014   **TOTAL LIQUOR** 8.8 GALLONS (33.5 LITERS)

MAKES 6 GALLONS (23 LITERS)	READY TO DRINK 5 WEEKS	ESTIMATED ABV 5.7%	BITTERNESS RATING 31.5 IBU	COLOR RATING 75.6 EBC

FOR THE MASH

LIQUOR 4 gallons (15 liters)   **MASH TIME** 1 hr   **TEMPERATURE** 20°F (68°C)

Grain bill	Quantity
Pale malt	8lb (4kg)
Flaked oats	2¼lb (1kg)
Chocolate malt	14oz (400g)
Special B malt	1lb 2oz (500g)
Carafa special III	5½oz (150g)

FOR THE BOIL

LIQUOR 7 gallons (27 liters)   **BOIL TIME** 1 hr 15 mins

Hops	Quantity	IBU	When to add
Magnum 11.6%	¾oz (20g)	29.3	At start of boil
Willamette 4.5%	¾oz (20g)	2.7	For last 10 mins of boil

Other			
Irish moss	1 tsp		For last 15 mins of boil

FERMENT

FERMENTATION 68°F (20°C)   **CONDITIONING** 4 weeks at 50°F (10°C)

Yeast
White Labs WLP800 Pilsner Lager

Description of Tropical Stout that is given in BJCP guidelines

Original gravity range suggested by BJCP is 1.056–1.075
Final gravity range suggested is 1.010–1.018
Total liquor is the total amount of water needed for the entire batch

ABV range suggested is 5.5–8.0 percent
Bitterness 30–50 IBU
Color 39–79 EBC

Liquor is the amount of water needed for the mash; it's calculated by multiplying total weight of malt by 2.5
Mash time of 1 hour is a standard mash length
Mash temperature is slightly increased for a sweeter finish

Pale malt is used as a base malt for many recipes
Flaked oats add mouthfeel and head retention
Chocolate malt adds color and chocolate character
Special B malt provides some sweetness and some dark fruit characters
Carafa special III provides the roast character without burnt harshness

Liquor is the total liquid needed in the boiler after the mash has been sparged
Boil time of 1 hr 15 mins is the standard boil length

Magnum hops are used for adding bitterness
Willamette hops enhance the fruitiness of the beer without adding too much hop character

Irish moss is a fining agent that helps clarify the beer (see p61)

Conditioning temperature used is warmer than for a typical lager yeast

Yeast chosen is a warm-fermenting lager yeast, as specified by BJCP

USEFUL INFORMATION

FREQUENTLY ASKED QUESTIONS

1) How can I increase the alcohol content of my beer?

The simple answer is: add more sugar. During fermentation, the yeast will ferment this additional sugar and produce additional alcohol as a by-product. It is best to use dried malt extract (DME) as your sugar source, since it will introduce additional alcohol without increasing the overall sweetness of the beer. It is important to bear in mind that the yeast will be able to effectively ferment only a certain amount of additional DME or sugar, so follow these guidelines for a 6-gallon (23-liter) batch:

- 1lb 2oz (500g) DME will increase the ABV by approximately 0.5%
- 2¼lb (1kg) DME will increase the ABV by approximately 1%
- 1lb 2oz (500g) brown sugar will increase the ABV by approximately 0.9%
- 1lb 2oz (500g) maple syrup will increase the ABV by approximately 0.7%
- 1lb 2oz (1kg) honey will increase the ABV by approximately 0.7%

2) Why is the original gravity (OG) lower than expected?

There are three likely causes for this:

- You have added too much water to a kit or malt-extract recipe. With full-mash recipes, a low OG may indicate that the mash efficiency is low.

- You have not stirred the wort properly after adding water to a kit or malt-extract recipe. This will leave all the sugars at the bottom of the fermenter, causing the gravity to be too low at the top.

- The prefermented wort was too cool or too hot when you took a gravity reading. Hydrometers are calibrated to take readings when the wort is at a set temperature—typically 68°F (20°C)—so if it is cooler or hotter than this, the results will be inaccurate.

3) How long will my beer keep for?

As long as the beer does not become oxidized once it has been bottled or barrelled, it should keep for several months. In fact, many styles will benefit from extended aging.

4) How do I know whether my beer has started to ferment?

A thick foam should form on top—usually within 24 hours of the yeast being pitched. This is completely normal and actually protects the beer during fermentation. The best way to check how fermentation is progressing is to take a hydrometer reading and see whether it is lower than the original gravity. If your beer hasn't started fermenting after 48 hours, check that it is at the correct temperature and adjust if necessary. If the temperature is correct, then you will need to pitch more yeast.

5) Why is my beer flat?

Flat beer is caused by either too little priming sugar being added prior to bottling or barrelling or because the priming sugar has not been able to ferment due to the storage temperature being incorrect. If you are storing your beer in a barrel, try adding carbon dioxide. If the beer is still flat, check for leaks around the cap.

CONVERSION CHART

Volume

The recipes in this book make approximately:
6 gallons (US) / 5 gallons (imperial) / 23 liters /
48 pints (US) / 40 pints (imperial)

To convert:

Fluid ounces (imperial) to liters:	divide by 35.195
Cups (US) to liters:	divide by 4.227
Pints (US) to liters:	divide by 2.11
Pints (imperial) to liters:	divide by 1.76
Gallons (US) to liters:	divide by 0.26
Gallons (imperial) to liters:	divide by 0.22

(To convert the other way, multiply by the figures shown.)

Weight

To convert:

Ounces to grams:	divide by 0.035
Pounds to kilograms:	divide by 2.205

(To convert the other way, multiply by the figures shown.)

Temperature

To convert:

°F to °C:	subtract 32, then divide by 1.8
°C to °F:	multiply by 1.8, then add 32

ONLINE FORUMS

www.homebrewersassociation.org
A forum hosted by the American
Homebrewers Association with plenty of
support for home brewers of all levels.

www.canadianhomebrewers.com
A great Canadian-based brewing forum well
suited for beginners.

www.homebrewtalk.com
A popular and friendly US-based home-
brewing forum.

forum.northernbrewer.com
A forum hosted by a home-brewing
company that offers very helpful advice.

USEFUL WEBSITES

www.bjcp.org
The Beer Judge Certification Program
provides guidelines for each beer style.

www.mrmalty.com
A useful brewing resource, especially for yeast
substitutions and yeast-starter calculations.

www.brewersfriend.com
A useful resource with calculators,
spreadsheets, and a recipe builder.

www.beersmith.com
Includes downloadable software plus lots
of additional brewing information.

www.beeralchemyapp.com
A downloadable application that creates
recipes and tracks your ingredient orders.

www.beerlabelizer.com
Provides a series of design templates that
allow you to customize and create your own
beer labels.

BREWING SOFTWARE

BeerSmith
Beer Alchemy

INDEX

INDEX

DK UK

Editor Toby Mann

US Editor Jennette ElNaggar

Senior Art Editor Barbara Zúñiga

Senior Jacket Creative Nicola Powling

Jacket Designer Amy Cox

Jackets Co-ordinator Lucy Philpott

Pre-Production Producer David Almond

Producer Samantha Cross

Creative Technical Support Sonia Charbonnier

Managing Editor Stephanie Farrow

Managing Art Editor Christine Keilty

Art Director Maxine Pedliham

Publishing Director Mary-Clare Jerram

DK INDIA

Pre-Production Manager Sunil Sharma

DTP Designer Pushpak Tyagi

Photography Haarala Hamilton

FOR THE 2013 EDITION

Senior Editor Bob Bridle

Senior Art Editor Heather Matthews

Managing Editor Dawn Henderson

Managing Art Editor Christine Keilty

Publisher Peggy Vance

This American Edition, 2019
First American Edition, 2013
Published in the United States by DK Publishing
1450 Broadway, Suite 801, New York, NY 10018

ABOUT THE AUTHOR

Greg Hughes is an experienced home brewer, a leading member of the home-brewing industry, and co-owner and founder of BrewUK, one of the UK's largest online home-brewing retailers and community websites. He also runs his own craft brewery, Dark Revolution. Greg organizes national competitions in conjunction with some of the UK's leading commercial breweries, and encourages home brewers of all levels to improve their craft through continued support and product development. With a wealth of experience in all areas of home brewing, Greg specializes in the production of innumerable styles of ales.

ACKNOWLEDGMENTS

For the 2019 edition

DK would like to thank: Wei Tang for prop styling; Daniel Ironside for reviewing the recipes in the US edition; Corinne Masciocchi for proofreading; and Marie Lorimer for creating the index.

For the 2013 edition

The author would like to thank: A huge thank you to my wife, Tanya, and children, Rico and Macy. Without their support during all those long hours spent creating beers in the garage, this book would never have been possible.

DK would like to thank: Phil Robins at Longdog Brewery for checking the recipes; Tony Briscoe and Ian O'Leary for photography; Wei Tang for prop styling; Kate Fenton for design assistance; and Chris Mooney and Elizabeth Clinton for editorial assistance.

All images © Dorling Kindersley
For further information see: **www.dkimages.com**

Warning: Please take care when following the instructions in this book, especially when boiling and transferring large quantities of liquids. The Publisher cannot accept responsibility for any accidents that may result from following the instructions contained in this book.